Affiliate Marketing 101

Volume Two in the Series

A Beginner's Guide to Internet Profits

by

Justin Southworth

Text Copyright © 2018
Justin Southworth
All rights reserved
Text may be reproduced in part with attribution to the author.

ISBN 978-1987492514

Legal Disclaimer

Before you scroll down and read anything in this eBook, you need to be fully aware of the following.

Income Disclaimer: This document contains business strategies, marketing methods and other business advice that, regardless of the results and experience of others, may not produce the same or even similar results for you. I make absolutely no guarantee, expressed or implied, that by following the advice contained herein you will make any money or improve your current profits, as there are an infinite number of factors and variables that come into play regarding any given business.

Primarily, results will depend on the nature of the product or business model, the conditions of the marketplace, and situations and elements that are beyond the control of the business operator. Then too, sadly, there is the operator of the business; ambition, intelligence, work ethic, experience of the individual, aversion to or propensity for risk—these factors and many more are part of the equation that results in failure or success or anything in between.

As with any business endeavor, you assume all risk related to operations, investment, and money based on your own discretion and at your own risk and expense.

Liability Disclaimer: By reading this document, you assume all risks associated with using the advice given below, with a full understanding that you, solely, are responsible for anything that may occur as a result of putting this information into action in any way, regardless of your interpretation of the advice.

You further agree that the author cannot be held responsible in any way for the success or failure of your business as a result of the information presented herein. It's your responsibility to conduct your own due diligence regarding the safe and successful operation of your business if you intend to apply any of the information contained in this book in any way to your business operations.

In summary, you understand that the author makes absolutely no guarantees regarding income as a result of applying this information, as well as the fact that you are solely responsible for the results of any action taken on your part as a result of this information. As with all books of advice, self-help, and information there is a basic, unstated agreement between author and reader: If you succeed wildly, I won't send you an additional bill to claim part of your profits; if you fail miserably, you won't send me a bill to cover your expenses. Fair deal? This book should be only one of a number of sources of education and training towards success in your business.

Now that we've got that out of the way, let's get on with the good stuff!

Contents

Legal Disclaimer 1

Contents 3

Preface 5

Affiliate Marketing 101: A Beginner's Guide 9

    Affiliate Sites 14

    Other Avenues 16

    ClickBank Dissected 22

    Choosing Your Products 28

Getting Started 31

    Traffic Generation 101 34

    Product Launch Shortcut 44

    A Word About Building Your Email List 51

    Things to Consider 59

    Other Ways of Building Links & Generating Traffic Instantly: 69

    Final Words 85

    Internet Marketing Glossary 87

Preface

Let's set the stage: Some people bought this book. If that's you, then thank you, muchas gracias, danke schön, merci beaucoup, and どうもありがとうございました. Others downloaded the free eBook. To you I also say thank you, muchas gracias, danke schön, merci beaucoup, and どうもありがとうございました.

Whether I made a buck or two from a sale, or you're someone who is interested enough in Internet marketing to have found my download site, it's all the same to me. I'm just glad you're here.

I could assume you know what affiliate marketing is, but then most people know what "assume" really means: making an "ass" out of "u" and "me." So I won't assume anything and start from the very beginning.

In the old days (as when I was a kid, way before the Internet), it was common for people to get a high school diploma and then decide whether to go into the "trades" or go on to college for a bachelor's or advanced degree. If you went into the trades, you might have become a tool and die maker. These are they guys (or gals if you'll excuse my political incorrectness) who make tools that make tools, machine tools, the bedrock of industry. Before you can manufacture a hammer to sell at Lowe's or Home Depot, someone has to make the die and the tools that turn metal, fiberglass, and wood into that hammer.

Why am I talking about tool and die makers in a book on affiliate marketing?

Let's back up a bit and I'll explain. Before the Internet there was direct (snail) mail and billboards and television advertising and magazine ads and other means of letting the public know you had a product that could make their life easier, more enjoyable, less painful, or with which they could make more money. With the advent of the Internet came a whole new way, a new paradigm if you will, of letting the public know you have something that might benefit them.

In the early days you only had to insert an ad in front of a page someone wanted to see, or flash a banner at the top of the page, or send an enticing email. Internet programming was rudimentary and spam was only some kind of animal and vegetable product in a can (and that's about as close to knowing what's in that infamous can as we're going to get). But as technology progressed it became more and more difficult to get your ad in front of the public because the number of web sites and amount of advertising increased exponentially every year. Letting the public know you had something of value became increasingly difficult.

Enter the tool and die makers of the Internet.

There are people who make tools to enable developers of Internet tools to bring their products to market. For example, to effectively market an application, say, a WordPress plugin, you need a HUGE list of email addresses of potential buyers.

How do you build that list?

You might have guessed—there's a software tool for that. It may be the greatest thing since the invention of the zipper, but until the Internet world knows about it, it's useless.

Enter the affiliate marketer.

The software developer who created that tool wants to let the world know about it. You, the affiliate marketer, become a business partner with the software developer and act as his or her manufacturer's representative. You, the affiliate marketer, have the expertise, the knowledge, the contacts, the email list, and the drive to get the word out to the world that there is a fantastic product to help other developers and people with something to sell let the world know about their product.

You, the affiliate marketer, are the bridge between the software geek and the buying public.

And in exchange for providing your invaluable service you make a hefty commission without having to endure some of the downsides of running a business:

- You don't have to handle any products.
- You don't have to ship anything.
- You don't have to provide customer support.
- You don't have to manage refunds.

And if that weren't enough, you can:

- Work from anywhere in the world with an internet connection.
- Work the hours you choose.
- Make as much money as your ambition and willingness to learn and innovate will allow.

But the life of an internet marketer, especially in the early stages, is not all fun and games. There's a lot to learn and for most people, the money doesn't come in as a deluge from your first day on the job. You have to have patience. You have to have persistence. You have to have an attitude that says you're going to make a success of this no matter what. You'll see uncountable advertisements that tell you you'll be making money with this or that program before nightfall, if you just follow the three simple steps outlined in this zip file for only $29.95.

Don't you believe it.

If it were that easy everyone would be doing it, and then there'd be no room for you. Right?

Be thankful this is not easy. But with the information contained in this book you can get a good start. By going through this information and really considering the information, looking at the web sites we refer to, and taking it step by step, you can avoid a lot of the sand traps that have swallowed up so many others.

Affiliate Marketing 101:
A Beginner's Guide

Welcome to the Affiliate Marketing 101, a guide written for affiliate marketers who are looking for a step-by-step blueprint to success in this fast-growing industry.

Affiliate marketing is one of the most popular methods that new marketers use to generate a full-time income online. And why not? As an affiliate marketer you are not required to develop your own product, you don't have to provide after-sale support, and in many cases you don't even need your own website.

Yes but, you might think, as an affiliate marketer you can't make as much money as the developer. My answer: maybe, maybe not. But think of it this way; someone who creates a software product or two or maybe three gets a higher percentage of the total income throughout the entire funnel, but the affiliate marketer can market five, ten, or fifteen products at any one time, depending on the amount of time he or she might choose to devote daily to setting up campaigns and finding new sources of customers. Plus, if one of those products turns out to not sell well, it's no big deal. The affiliate marketer can easily find another product to promote, and another, and another until he or she hits a winner.

It's not a panacea, but it's as close to it as you are likely to find. If you can devote two or three hours a day to your business you can eventually build an income stream that will allow you to make a good living solely from affiliate marketing. Not only that, but you can do it from anywhere in the world where you can find a reliable Internet connection.

So, what exactly is affiliate marketing and how can you join the ranks of those who are earning a decent income every single day in this exciting market?

Here's a brief summary of what affiliate marketing really is:

An affiliate marketer is one who promotes someone else's product for a monetary commission. And what is the product? We're normally talking software solutions for eCommerce, products that do not require physical shipment. Software applications are downloaded by the purchaser over the Internet. For example, someone might have an Amazon.com affiliate store and needs a way to promote his business and capture email addresses for his weekly newsletter. The affiliate marketer has an agreement with a software developer to market a product that does just this function in exchange for a commission. The affiliate marketer's challenge is to let people with a need for the product know, one, that the product exists and two, where to buy it. In exchange for linking the potential buyer with the software developer, the affiliate marketer earns a commission when a sale is made. Sometimes this payment is given in the form of a flat rate, (e.g., $10.00

per sale), other times the payment is a percentage of the sale price. Note also that sometimes the payment is immediate, other times the payment is delayed as sales are frequently made on the basis of a money-back guarantee within, for example, thirty days. To ensure the money is available for distribution to the affiliate marketer, the commission payment may be delayed until after the warranty period.

While the affiliate marketer does his job of finding customers and selling the product the software developer can be developing new products and supporting the products already sold. The software developer, the affiliate marketer, and the customer all benefit from the arrangement.

Generally, affiliates generate revenue only by selling the product. (Other methods of earning commissions are discussed later on.) Product promotion is accomplished by advertising on blogs, websites, directories, classified ads, and by building the marketer's own list and sending out targeted email campaigns to list members. Websites on which the affiliate can promote products are typically social networking sites such as Facebook, Twitter, and Squidoo or are marketed via Google+ and other paid advertising sites.

With the possibility of any one of hundreds of millions of Internet users reaching a site where they can purchase a software solution, how does the developer know who is responsible for a particular customer? What or who led that customer to the sales page? When you register as an affiliate for a product you'll be given a unique identification number that will be attached to the link the user clicks on to get to the product page. Software code built into the sales page will then be able to identify the person responsible for sending the traffic. If the customer makes a purchase, the affiliate marketing software links the purchase to the person who brought the customer to the seller. That marketer's payment instructions have been entered into the system so payment can be made.

Software developers normally use affiliate networks such as ClickBank and JVZoo to track affiliate marketers. These sites are well-established and reputable. Their systems keep track of offers, affiliates, and clicks to sales pages, sales, and commissions. Typically on these sites, the affiliate marketer can also add a free bonus to the sale to encourage potential buyers to purchase through his or her link, as more than one affiliate marketer (usually many) will be promoting any one product.

With ClickBank, JVZoo, and other affiliate tracking systems, an affiliate simply creates one account and then can gain access to a wide array of products and services offered through that site. The registration process may be virtually instantaneous, or approval may take some days, depending on the software developer's preferences. The registration and product request process will be covered later.

On merchant (software developer) websites that run their own in-house affiliate programs, affiliate marketers will create individual accounts on each site.

The site will provide some or all promotional media including but not limited to banners, advertisements, pre-written blog posts, forum signatures, classified ad material, press release documentation, and even specific keywords to target visitors through advertising circuits like Google Adsense or AdBrite.

Affiliate networks, such as ClickBank, JVZoo, or Commission Junction process payments, release payment to affiliates, and serve as a go-between for merchants (developers) and marketing partners (affiliates).

Depending on the affiliate network and the developer, commissions vary. The affiliate marketer will always want to pay attention to the product cost, the commission percentage on the first product as well as other products in the sales funnel. For a product that has had sales, the affiliate should also look at past conversion rates to indicate the desirability of the product prior to spending time setting up campaigns or putting in the effort, to say nothing of the money, to advertise.

As in any business, receiving payment for services rendered is a paramount concern. When beginning an affiliate marketing business, it is strongly suggested that the marketer only deal with an affiliate network that is well established. Due diligence is the word of the day. For that reason, we suggest narrowing your affiliate network selection to the major players—ClickBank, JVZoo, and those listed below. There are many others, but until you have some experience it is wise to stick with these agents.

Affiliate Sites

To help you get familiar with the popular affiliate networks currently available online, here is a quick overview of a handful of the ones most widely used:

ClickBank (https://www.clickbank.com/)

One of the most popular affiliate networks, ClickBank offers free affiliate accounts (merchant accounts are $50). Setting up your affiliate account is very easy. We'll discuss this site in more detail below.

Commission Junction (cj.com)

Otherwise known as "CJ.com", Commission Junction has been around for many years and has a reputation for on time payments and very good support. CJ.com also features hundreds of merchants from every niche market or subject, giving you a wide variety of products to promote.

Commission Junction works a bit differently from Clickbank with respect to acceptance of affiliate marketers. While ClickBank allows merchants total control of affiliate approval, CJ.com maintains some control over the affiliate approval process. If you're new to affiliate marketing, CJ.com might not be the best affiliate network to approach.

As opposed to CJ.com, ClickBank allows you to choose which products to promote and instantly generate your affiliate link without the requirement of the merchant reviewing your website or approving your registration.

Commission Junction enables their merchants to selectively choose who is allowed to participate in each affiliate program, so if you are new to affiliate marketing, you may end up a bit frustrated when you are turned down due to your website not receiving enough traffic or being focused on specific topics.

Pay Dot Com (http://paydotcom.com/)

PayDotCom was created by Mike Filsaime and is similar to ClickBank in terms of product marketplace and niche coverage. An advantage of Pay Dot Com over ClickBank is that rather than wait every two weeks for a paycheck to be released via postal mail, as ClickBank.com offers, PayDotCom.com delivers affiliate commissions directly into your PayPal account daily. At this time, only those who have a PayPal account are able to participate as either a merchant or affiliate within this network.

Share A Sale (http://shareasale.com/)

ShareASale.com started quite a few years ago when there were fewer merchants using their services. The affiliate had fewer choices of products to promote, necessarily making it more difficult to find high quality products.

These days, things have changed. ShareASale.com has grown into an extensive affiliate marketplace, and since all merchants registered with them are required to retain a cash balance of funds to pay affiliates, it's a risk-free way to ensure that you are paid for all of your efforts.

ShareASale, like ClickBank and PayDotCom, handle all payments on behalf of the merchants. While ShareASale enables merchants to manually approve affiliates as CJ.com does, from my own personal experience approval has been very quick and easy.

Link Share (http://www.LinkShare.com)

Link Share is an ever-growing affiliate marketplace and with it comes a great variety of lucrative and high paying affiliate opportunities.

Other Avenues

While this book deals with affiliate marketing along the lines of marketing someone else's software for a commission, other forms of earning money bear mention that are closely related. We won't go into detail on these other forms of marketing, but there are endless sources of information should any of these appeal to you.

CPA Networks
Apart from being paid per sale, there are online networks available to you that pay for simply generating traffic, regardless of purchases. These are termed Cost per Action, or CPA networks. CPA is a good way to supplement your income as an affiliate marketer; many

new marketers find it easier to generate a lead or a click, than to encourage visitors to become a paid customer. These CPA programs often offer payments on a flat rate basis or a percentage platform.

Pay per Lead

These sites generally pay for information such as names, email address, and location, as well as other demographic details.

Pay per Click

These programs pay you for every click to a specified landing or squeeze page as designated by the merchant.

Pay per Sign Up

These programs pay you for every sign-up, typically for an offer or for confirmed and unique auto-responder email list subscriptions.

Pay per Download

Software developers will often pay you to generate traffic for trial downloads or demo copies of their software with the hope that the user will upgrade to a paid version after the trial time period has expired.

There are more CPA networks than you can possibly utilize. Again, these networks act as a middleman between you and the merchant and require registration and approval.

Following are a few of the popular CPA networks online:

AzoogleAds (http://www.AzoogleAds.com)

This is one of the more popular CPA networks, consistently growing in size. Established in 2000, it's known to be one of the more reliable networks, offering payouts per lead, per sale, and per download. They have a consolidated payment via check for a minimum of $50.00, with stats and data appearing in real time on their website.

MaxBounty (http://www.MaxBounty.com)

Simple registration and guaranteed acceptance makes Max Bounty a popular program within communities and online forums based on CPA networking. This is another company that has been active for long enough to have proven themselves reliable, with good customer support and timely payout. You can set your payment minimum to an amount ranging from their minimum of $50 up to $200, with payments disbursed monthly via check, bank transfer, or PayPal.

International members are also permitted to join with special promotions and campaigns that target those groups.

Never Blue Ads (http://www.NeverBlueAds.com)

This network offers a large variety of different campaigns, with a focus on Pay per Lead programs. With over twenty categories chock full of viable and lucrative offers, there is no shortage of programs to promote. Payout is monthly with a minimum requirement of only $25.00. On the registration form the only form of payment available is a mailed check. However once you are a member you can contact your affiliate representative for additional options, including PayPal. Registration is simple and approval is quick. Confirmation is received normally within two business days.

Offers Quest (http://www.OffersQuest.com)

This is a smaller network but is growing in popularity. Their focus is primarily on Cost per Lead campaigns. However, before you can be approved for membership you must have a fully functional website that is already generating a bit of traffic. The website must be in English. One other caveat to note: members are not permitted to offer incentives to visitors. Payouts are monthly via PayPal or check with a minimum balance requirement of $20.00 for those within the United States or Canada, or $50.00 for other countries.

Copeac (http://www.Copeac.com)

This network offers a variety of action based programs including: Cost per Sale, Cost per Click, Cost per Acquisition, and Cost per Lead, with many categories available and a referral program offering an additional two percent commission for new advertiser sign-ups. Payment is made monthly via bank wire or check with a minimum requirement of $100.00. They also offer a 24-hour emergency hotline if you need help at any time.

During registration, you will be required to verify your location using their automated telephone verification system (similar to the system that PayPal uses).

Rocket Profit (http://www.RocketProfit.com)

This is one of my favorite networks, due to their extremely wide scope in terms of unique Cost per Lead and Cost per Sale offers. Payment is available via bank wire, PayPal, and check with a minimum requirement of only $25.00, disbursed every two weeks.

Applications are reviewed daily, with notification of acceptance received within two to three business days.

Hydra Network (http://www.HydraNetwork.com)

This is a widely popular CPA network featuring Cost per Click, Cost per Lead, and Cost per Sale offers. At the time of this writing, they offer the highest payouts of any of the mentioned CPA programs. Hydra offers a large assortment of promotional media as well, including email campaigns, co-registration, and search.

They also provide very detailed statistics and reporting, making it easy for you to monitor your progress in real-time with pre-screening of campaign matches available to ensure that you choose the best campaigns to match your existing audience and traffic sources.

Hydra Network disburses payments every fifteen days via bank deposit (wire) and PayPal.

Modern Click (http://www.ModernClick.com)

This program is very difficult to get into, as they manually approve every applicant. However, once you are accepted you will find plenty of lucrative campaigns to work with and access to advanced tracking tools and real-time statistics.

The minimum payout is $25, paid monthly via check or PayPal.

Their registration process is a bit tedious and lengthy but approval is quick.

Direct Leads (http://www.DirectLeads.com)

This program features a solid program with a wide scope of available offers.

Web Sponsors (http://www.WebSponsors.com)

This is one of the larger affiliate networks. Their featured offers are lucrative and high quality products make promoting very easy.

There are dozens of other CPA networks online with new ones springing up daily. Some of these companies will offer you the ability to feature coupon codes on your website, which prompt visitors to check for new savings frequently boosting traffic to your website and providing a useful service for potential customers.

Others will offer direct content and pre-written ad copy. The more savvy ones will offer you the ability to generate revenue from 404 Error pages by splashing their pre-made squeeze page graphics throughout areas of your website not regularly used. This is an extra way of generating additional revenue with absolutely no effort on your part.

ClickBank Dissected

Since Clickbank is one of the largest and most popular affiliate marketplaces, and makes the startup process incredibly easy, let's take a closer look at the program. If you choose ClickBank you'll be able to establish your business and earn daily revenue from their offers quickly.

To begin, visit http://www.ClickBank.com. Click on the "Sign Up" link in the top navigation bar to get started.

The ClickBank sign up page will require a bit of information about you. (They're going to be representing you and handling money—would you expect otherwise?) Pay particular attention to the name and address associated with your new account; after setup these can only be changed by writing to a Clickbank representative and mannually requesting modifications. The address that you supply within the sign-up page is where your affiliate checks will be sent, so double check this information and be sure that it's accurate.

Fill out the form entirely, choosing a short and memorable account nickname. Your nickname, or account ID, will be attached to your affiliate link. You want to be careful to choose something generic if you plan to market different products in a variety of niche marketplaces.

Where shall we send your checks?

Country:*	UNITED STATES
Payee Name:*	
Street / PO Box:*	
Suite or Apt #:	
City:*	
State / Province:*	ALABAMA
Zip / Post Code:*	

How can we contact you?

Your first name:*	
Your last name:*	
Your email address (example: joe@aol.com):*	
Your phone number (required!):*	ext:
Address of your web site (if any):	

Select a nickname for your new account

Account Nickname ‡ (5-10 letters & digits):*	
Check here to receive targeted, account specific promotions from ClickBank via email:	☐

For example, if you are planning to promote products in the "make money niche" as well as the "lose weight" niche, you'll want to choose an account name that is not specific to either field. You should also avoid words such as "sell" and "promote" as those who click on your links will see the keywords you have chosen to use in your ID.

Also note that ClickBank limits your account nickname to only ten characters or fewer. You may have to get creative.

After completing your account registration details, ClickBank will automatically generate a password for you. You used to be able to choose your own but for the last couple of years, they have their system set up to assign a unique one for each affiliate. We can guess that many user-generated passwords were weak, creating security problems for the company. Whatever the reason, make sure you document the password in some fashion because it will not be easy to remember. ClickBank will not automatically send your password to you via email after registration, so make note if it <u>immediately</u> when it's assigned.

After you have set up your Clickbank account, your affiliate link will look something like this:

http://*Your-ID*.publisher.hop.clickbank.net

Don't worry about the link containing ClickBank.*net* rather than ClickBank.*com*. That's just part of an internal process that will not affect your business or commissions.

The "publisher" within your links will change depending on the product you're promoting. For an example of product names, click on the *Marketplace* link at the top of the ClickBank home page to view the many different products that you can choose from.

http://www.ClickBank.com/marketplace.htm

Here is where the fun begins. The ClickBank marketplace features products and services within categories and sub-categories, making it easy for you to selectively browse specific topics or niche market material. This can save you a lot of time if you are looking to find new products that are focused on specific topics.

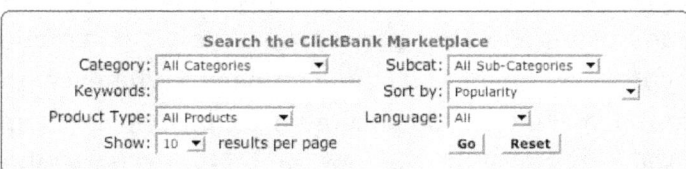

To start, in the *Category* box, select your interest. You can also type in specific keywords or choose a sub-category to narrow the search results.

After you have set up your search query, click on *Go* to load the results window.

In my example below, I have chosen to search through the *Health & Fitness* category, and *Beauty* sub category, with no keywords entered, sorting by *Popularity*.

> 1) Chopper-Tattoo - Top Tattoo Offer ! The #1 Tattoo Gallery On The Web. Converting Like Crazy! Pays 75%, Affiliates Must See. Free Music Downloads With Membership Allows Creative Marketing. New Affiliate Tracking In Email, Exit Ad, & Google Upon Request: Chopper-tattoo.com/affiliates/.
> $/sale: $20.28 | Future $: - | Total $/sale $20.28 | %/sale: 75.0% | %refd: 95.0% | grav: 201.09
> view pitch page | create hoplink
>
> 2) Tattoo Me Now - Completely New Design - Conversions Up 116%! New Higher Price Points. Earn 75% Of $27 Or $37. -- Tattoos - One Of The Largest Markets Online. The Phrase Tattoos Is Consistently Ranked In The Top 10 Most Searched Keywords. 2c Clicks In Google Are Still Available! TattooMeNow.com/affiliates.
> $/sale: $19.12 | Future $: - | Total $/sale $19.12 | %/sale: 75.0% | %refd: 76.0% | grav: 152.78
> view pitch page | create hoplink

From the results window you will see a description of each available product along with a line of (green, if you're viewing the page and not the B&W eBook text) text that includes things like $/sale, Future $, Total $/sale, etc.

What do these elements mean?

- $/sale: The amount of money you earn for each sale.
- Future $: Average rebill revenue.
- Total $/sale: Average total $ per sale, including all rebills.
- %/sale: The percentage of the product sale price that the sale represents.
- %/refd: Fraction of publisher's total sales that are referred by affiliates.

- Grav: The measure of how many affiliates are promoting the product.

For each affiliate paid in the last eight weeks Clickbank adds an amount between 0.1 and 1.0 to the total. The more recent the last referral, the higher the value added.

The Gravity (grav) indicator will tell you how well a product is selling. So a gravity score of 100 means a product is selling better than one with a gravity score of, for example, 20.

Looking at your search results, you can easily choose a product that you wish to promote. In order to generate your unique affiliate link, you could click on the link titled *Generate Hoplink*. Clicking here will open a window that asks you to enter in your ClickBank username. This is the ID that you chose earlier when you registered for an account.

ClickBank NickName:

Tracking ID (Optional):

Create

Enter in your ClickBank Nickname and click "Create" to generate a unique ClickBank affiliate link. This link is what you use to direct traffic to the offer with your affiliate ID embedded. When(!) the product is purchased, ClickBank will know whom to pay for the referral.

Note: You can also track your affiliate campaigns by entering a unique tracking ID (something you will identify or remember). Here is an explanation of the Tracking ID and how it works, according to the ClickBank website:

> *As an affiliate, the tracking code enhancement provides the power to track and manage your campaigns by tying a specific sale back to the promotion that initiated it.*
>
> *The tracking code is implemented throughout the ClickBank system as "tid". The format of the hoplink URL with a tracking code is located below.*

http://AFFILIATE.PUBLISHER.hop.clickbank.net/?tid=ZZZZZ

In order for the feature to work properly, you must adhere to these standards during its implementation. The tracking code value, which is *zzzzz* in the example above, can be up to eight alpha-numeric characters long. Any value longer than eight characters will be truncated. Any value containing characters other than alpha or numeric values will have the entire tracking code value removed from the *hoplink* and the order process and will not show in the transaction report. Tracking code values in lower case characters will be set to all uppercase. The tracking code parameter, which is *tid* in the example above, must be lower case.

You can also view the merchant's sales page by clicking on *view pitch page*.

Choosing Your Products

To maximize your profits as an affiliate marketer, you need to learn how to choose products most likely to perform well—a euphemism for *sell like hotcakes and make you a ton of money*. You'll want to market products that are in demand, easy to sell, and pay a high commission.

Thankfully, there are resources available that will help both new and seasoned affiliate marketers select winning products from among the hundreds featured within the marketplace. Here's two:

- CB Engine, http://www.cbengine.com
- CB Trends, http://www.CBTrends.com

Let's take a closer look at these two resources and learn exactly how they can instantly help you choose the best products based on your market.

CB Trends is a free ClickBank research and analytics tool that allows ClickBank affiliates to track the performance history of Marketplace-listed products. According to CBTrends, *promoting products listed in Marketplace without verifying their performance history can lead to wasted funds and disappointment. Many people who are just starting with ClickBank affiliate marketing fail because they start promoting ClickBank products without verifying their performance history first*. This web application offers information regarding product performance, including the history of specific products within that marketplace. On the site, enter the vendors

ID (which you can find from within the ClickBank marketplace) and the CB Trends search engine will load relevant data associated with that product. This information can include popularity breakdown, gravity, earnings per sale, percent per sale, and referrals and commission earnings over a period of time.

By browsing the different graphs that will appear after each search, you can analyze the different aspects of each product including overall popularity, how well the product has done in the past, how many affiliates are promoting the product, and other factors important in deciding whether you want to spend time (and money?) promoting this product.

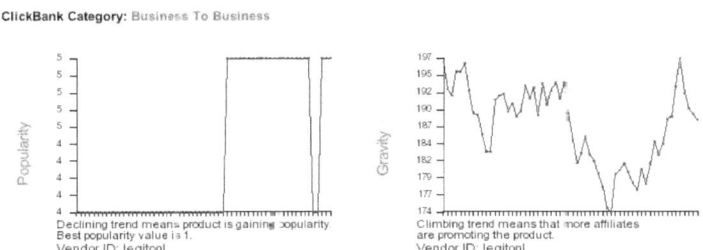

While dissecting this data isn't completely intuitive if you are a new affiliate marketer, as you continue to promote products and detect which ones are doing better in terms of conversion, you will begin to better understand the information available or sites like CBTrends and use it to your advantage in creating better, higher converting campaigns. As with everything in life, this is a learning process. There are so many tools and so much information available throughout the internet, part of the process is learning where to find the data you need and how to interpret it so that you can make intelligent decisions for your business.

CB Engine also offers a free search utility, very much the same as CB Trends. However, CB Engine requires a membership priced at $39.95 for a year's access to graphics, stats and history tracking. Before deciding whether you want to sign up for a membership you can take a 7-day test drive. It's worth noting, however, that in order to make the most of a free 7-day test, you need to know what you are testing and some familiarity with the data and information you can find on the site. (Would it do you any good to take a test drive of a car if you didn't know how to drive?)

Getting Started

Affiliate marketing is not different from any other business in the respect that you need to know how to manage daily operations and have the information at hand to make intelligent business decisions in order to stay in business and make a profit. You will need to learn how to properly manage your campaigns, stay focused and organized and always design a strategy before you begin to promote each product.

For instance, while a website or blog isn't required, it certainly makes the job easier in terms of having a landing page to send visitors to in order to direct them to multiple affiliate products you tend to promote. You'll also want to use a blog and/or website as a way of generating leads through an autoresponder such as Aweber.com (my personal preference).

By creating a mailing list of people interested in specific products or services, you can easily send out an advertisement containing your affiliate link whenever you want to. Everyone in affiliate marketing knows, the money is in the list.

An autoresponder account costs between $15 and $25 a month but is a worthwhile investment. I spent untold time manually promoting products before I ever decided to take advantage of the power that a mailing list provides and when I finally got started generating leads and creating targeted lists, I was able to easily triple my income literally overnight.

Unless you have some education in HTML, CSS, JavaScript, ASP, and other web design technologies, designing a website isn't easy. Even if you have all that training, your website can still suck unless you have some artistic talent. Outsourcing these projects can be costly and there's no guarantee you'll get a decent product in the end.

Thankfully, there is an easy solution to this problem.

One of several web page design tools is WordPress. It has its difficulties, but it also has more help available than you can shake a stick at to answer any questions you might have concerning how to manage your choice of countless of web page templates.

WordPress began as a blog platform, but it has evolved into a complete web application platform for not only blog sites, but full-blown e-commerce sites. Many high-quality templates are provided free of charge when you install WordPress, and WordPress itself is free and is available with a one-click install on many hosting sites, including my favorite, GoDaddy.com. You can easily find the perfect theme for your blog regardless of what niche market you are focused on within the hundreds of free theme directories online. You simply upload the theme into your WordPress admin area, and you're good to go.

You can also purchase WordPress templates (premade designs for your web site). With a purchased site you usually have greater access to support. If you're brand new to designing and building a web site, especially with

WordPress, this isn't a bad way to go; until you get the hang of it, WordPress can be somewhat confusing. And don't forget that old-fashioned thing, the paper book. You can pick up a copy of WordPress for Dummies used for under $10.00. Don't bother with the eBook version when you need a reference book like this. The ability to have a ready access to information by flipping pages back and forth is worth the extra expense. And forget about the cheap eBooks on WordPress. In my experience, these leave much to be desired. They're usually written quickly and poorly. Spend the extra money and get a high-quality book from a publisher you can trust. I don't personally care for the "For Dummies" moniker, but the series is reliable. If you're so inclined, you can also find all the information you will ever need at the WordPress website at http://www.WordPress.org. Go through their five-minute quick installation guide to get started. When you're ready to customize your website, you can browse through the free themes at the WordPress site, http://Wordpress.org/extend/themes, and find even more at these sites:

- http://themes.Wordpress.net
- http://www.FreeWPThemes.net
- http://www.SkinPress.com
- http://www.ThemeLab.com

In order to host WordPress, you will need an affordable hosting account. I personally recommend using www.GoDaddy.com as they are easy to use, affordable, and their customer service is second to none. Especially for those new to setting up web hosting, good customer service is invaluable.

GoDaddy.com is also where you'll register your domain name. Choose something that reflects your business if at all possible and similar to your affiliate site (ClickBank, JVZoo, etc.) name. Unless you plan to promote only one type of product on your website, you will need a domain name that could easily be used for multiple niche markets. Don't choose a domain name that's so specific you have no room to diversify your product line in the future. HotPoint was a great name for a company that manufactured ovens and stoves; once they branched out into refrigerators it wasn't so appropriate.

Ninety-nine percent of the time you'll find the domain name you would like is already registered. Keep thinking. Use your imagination. You'll come up with something that makes sense and isn't taken. If the name you really can't live without is already taken, you may be able to buy it. I registered a business name I no longer use, so as long as I have the rights to the name, if someone else wants it I'll sell it to them at a reasonable price.

Traffic Generation 101

So, you have a brandable domain name that is easy to remember, you have an affiliate account, and you have registered your domain name and set up a website.

So, what's the next step in our journey to affiliate marketing success?

Traffic!

Traffic!

And More Traffic!!!

Without traffic the best web site in the world is useless. So, how do you generate traffic to your website affordably, or better yet,

FREE?

There are countless ways to send an instant rush of traffic to your website at no cost. These methods often referred to as guerilla marketing. They take a bit of work, but they yield results if done correctly and if you stick with it.

The first method, although not the most efficient, is through SEO, Search Engine Optimization. The problem with relying solely on SEO is that it isn't a quick way of harnessing traffic. It's something you have to do, but optimizing your website or blog can take days, weeks, or even months to actually begin ranking at all, let alone ranking well for specific keywords. Depending on the competition, it can take an awful lot of detailed editing of every page of your site to boost your ranking. When you have optimized your site for SEO, it will still take time for the search engines to find and begin to rank your site on the first page of results.

Since this guide is an introduction and not, admittedly, the be-all and end-all of affiliate marketing training resources, we'll limit the discussion of SEO but leave you with several links to valuable resources you'll want to check out.

Since the vast, vast majority of searches are conducted through Google, we'll limit our discussion to that platform.

Keep in mind that Google, through whatever artificial intelligence they have created, search the Internet for sites that contain high quality information to satisfy any and all queries. Their search through the web is called, to continue the web image, crawling, as a spider crawls around a web. Google will crawl your website, cataloging its content and using proprietary, highly secret algorithms to gauge quality and originality of information. Among important criteria Google will use to evaluate whether you have relevant content is the number of links to and from your site, weighting the evaluation partly based on the relative quality of sites that link to yours. In other words, even if you have many links to your web site from other sites, but no one ever visits those sites and Google has determined their content is of poor quality or is not original, your site won't get any points.

Other criteria Google uses to determine your site's rank are how long visitors remain on your site once they go there. Even if your site is found in a Google search, if the visitor goes there and quickly leaves, you get no points.

Google will measure the load speed of your site and give you more credit for faster load time. This is why you don't want to weigh your site down with slow-loading, huge graphics and animation. (An additional note—regardless of search engine ranking, slow load time and heavy graphics create an extremely bad user experience, which will drive viewers away even if they do find our site and even if you have good information there. Keep your pages simple and clean, and keep your graphics as small in size (in megabytes) as possible.)

One final point, if your content is nothing but a summary of that on other sites, Google will not rank your site highly. There are a few popular sites that are nothing more than digests of news from other sites, but successful ones are rare and the sites from which they acquire their information will be the ones that Google will rank on their search page.

Find more information on competitive keywords in the tools listed below.

- Moz Keyword Difficulty and SERP Analysis Tool
- SEMRush Keyword Difficulty Tool
- Serpiq
- Canirank
- Colibri.io
- Seoprofiler
- Ultimatenichefinder
- Advanced Webranking's Keyword Difficult Tool
- Backlinko's in-depth guide

This post at http://www.seonick.net/rank-potential/ by Nick Eubanks will also help you understand site ranking so you can better determine useful keywords for your blog posts and other pages.

Key SEO components (reword this section – taken from another site)

- The page is constructed simply with no impediments to search crawlers
- Content offers everything a searcher might want in a unique high-quality amalgamation
- Clear layout, solid visuals,
- Like, tweet, and Google +1 buttons make the page easy to share.
- Primary and secondary search words appear in prominent positions in the headline, title, and content.
- Works on every size screen
- Meta data – authorship, description, schema markup

In addition to the time it takes to rank well at times, you also have to deal with the overload of professional, paying Google advertisers who place those ads that appear in the right hand column on your search results page. These advertisers pay for every click on their ads. Naturally, Google and other search engines are going to favor these guys over you. As they say, *money talks and BS walks*. Unless you have the funds to create your own paid campaigns to compete against them, you'll just have to accept second class status.

That doesn't mean that you have to throw in the towel, and it doesn't mean that you can't compete in the Internet marketplace. It does mean that you have to educate yourself and keep up with changes in the industry, as would any business person in any sort of enterprise. Search algorithms are constantly changing and someone is always coming up with a new way to get a page in front of an interested browser. You should always be on the lookout for new and better tools and methods, but keeping SEO on the front burner is a fact of the Internet marketer's life.

So, let's take a closer look at how you can optimize your website and rank in the Mother of All Search Engines, Google.

This section will necessarily be only an introduction to a primer on Search Engine Optimization. Search the Internet on SEO and you'll find enough information to keep you busy for a year, and that's just getting started. People make careers of being SEO experts. But the basics are fairly straightforward.

It's important to note that SEO's importance is relative to the product you're promoting. If your web site sells, for example, baby elephant diapers, SEO is going to be important to you. You probably won't be running ads on social media sites, but instead relying on people actively looking for what you have to sell. They'll go to Google or another search engine and type in baby elephant diapers. Making sure your web site text and graphics are optimized to enable search engines to find it is vital to your success.

On the other hand, if you're an affiliate marketer of software products, SEO isn't going to benefit you very much. There are millions of ads being displayed on computer and iPhone screens already—if someone want to know about a product to help him gather more email addresses, he won't have to search for it. This doesn't mean you don't need to be concerned with SEO, it just means that the time and effort you put into designing you site and crafting your text isn't nearly as important as if you were marketing a more esoteric product.

With that said, let's get started. The most important aspects of ranking in Google and other search engines is how well you craft your keywords. You want to make sure that you are using the very best keywords you can, those that are most relevant to your website or the products that you plan to promote and that the general user might search on. Thus, here in the United States, if you're marketing umbrellas, you wouldn't need to include *bumbershoot* in your keyword list. However, given the fact that Spanish is the second language of these states, you probably would want to include *paraguas*.

These keywords will be placed within your website's title tags, so if you were promoting a product called "Overnight Wealth", you would want to include "Overnight Wealth" in the title tag of the page that provides information about this product (and course, features your affiliate link).

One of the best ways to generate affiliate commissions is through review or rating based websites and we'll cover that in more detail later on, but just as an example, if I were reviewing a product called "Dog Training Secrets," the keywords I would include within the title tag of that landing page would be "Dog Training Secrets." Not "Dog Secrets." Not "Training Secrets," but the full product name, "Dog Training Secrets," spaced in individual keywords just like the product name would be on the front cover of a book and as a person looking for that would type into a search engine dialogue box.

You add your title into the source of your page or if you are using WordPress, you simply log into your admin panel and change the name of your blog to one that is based on specific keywords. WordPress will automatically update every page and post with this keyword title.

The title tag however isn't the only aspect of on-site SEO. There are other elements, equally as important including:

Page Title: Be sure to place your keyword within the page title itself.

Page Headings: The first line or two on your website is your page heading, usually larger than your body text, and is the first thing visitors to your website see. While you want your page heading to captivate them and prompt further reading, you also want to ensure that your keywords are included within your page heading.

Top, Middle and Bottom of your page.

Ensure that your keywords are spread throughout your content or article, but don't over-saturate (keyword stuff) your content. Search engines watch for this and will downgrade your site if they see it. As a rule of thumb, ensure that your keyword density never rises above five percent, otherwise search engines may penalize you for keyword stuffing. And don't use tricks like loading your page with hidden keywords—white font on a white background. That old trick has been used and abused and the search engines will laugh at you as they throw your site into the fiery depths of hell. Other tricks are just as dangerous. If you're reading even a year-old book about how to fool search engines to rank your page at the top of their lists, you're in the search engine dark ages and wasting your time.

Craft your article so that you weave your keywords throughout your copy. As with everything in life, balance is best. It's not easy or necessarily natural, but then that's why people who can write good copy, optimized for search engines, are well-paid for what they do.

If you want to be certain of your keyword density, you can use the free tool available at http://www.live-keyword-analysis.com to evaluate your copy. Just copy and paste your text into the box, enter up to three keywords and the script will detect the keyword density of your document, instantly. There are also plugins for WordPress that will do this for you. I, personally, use Yoast, but there are others. Take some time to go through the help files for whichever product you use and you'll learn as much as you need to know to get started.

Of course, another aspect of writing good keyword-based article content that the search engine will eat up like candy is ensuring that your content is fresh, relevant, and unique. Whether you re-write an existing article, purchase private label right (PLR) content or hire a freelance writer, make absolutely certain that your content is as unique as possible.

If you do go with pre-written content, be sure to change the information by at least 40%, preferably 60% or more if you can. Re-writing existing information is not difficult and even if you are unsure about the topic or know little about the subject, you only have to spend an hour conducting online research by browsing existing websites, article directories, and blogs to compile the information you need. Then, use the PLR article or book as an outline or framework and go through each sentence, changing the verbiage to match your personal style. Also, expand on ideas presented that you feel need more explanation. Along the way, if you're not an expert in the topic, you'll greatly expand your knowledge. You'll end up re-writing the article or book and have something of your own. Many affiliate marketers and even mainstream article authors do precisely this to produce new content and fresh ideas.

Not a great writer? When you've done your best with your re-write, put your article through the paces at CopyScape.com. This tool will check for uniqueness so you'll know whether you're publishing original, high-quality content.

Yoast, the SEO WordPress plugin mentioned above, will also check for readability, evaluating your article for vocabulary, grammar, sentence length, and other variables. An article that's stylistically difficult to read or has grammar problems won't be read. Period. Why waste your time?

One last thing we'll cover regarding on-site SEO is the use of anchor-based text links. These are links that show specific keywords rather than a URL to a site. For example, rather than include a URL in your text, such as http://www.AffiliateShortcut.com, use a hyperlinked keyword (text) anchor text, such as Discover Affiliate Shortcuts that is then hyperlinked to the URL.

Be sure to use anchor based links whenever possible— within your copy and content and when linking to your site on directories, classifieds, or other blogs.

Product Launch Shortcut

Whenever a developer launches a new product people rush to it in droves to buy it. This is great if you're one of the affiliates to offer it. But many (many, many) other marketers are vying to get their share of the sales in competition with you. Some have extensive mailing lists and have ready bonuses and freebies to offer in exchange for the prospect signing up through their link rather than yours.

New products are where the excitement is. This is not to say that a high-quality product can't be very profitable for you down the road, but you'll want to develop a plan for getting in on product launches or lose a lot of income opportunity.

That begs the question: how do you find out about these? One way to stay current on product launches is to subscribe to free JV (joint venture) websites. These communities will not only alert you to the newest product launches but often give you inside access and pre-launch sneak peeks at the products. In some cases, you can get a review copy absolutely free.

Because these product launches last only a short time and the excitement around them quickly dies down, you have to have a plan in place so that you can act fast. Being on a distribution list that instantly notifies you of an upcoming product launch is the only way to really stay on top of what is about to be released.

You can join JV Notify Pro at http://www.JVNotifyPro.com for free, but the free account is limited. To get all the benefits you'll need to subscribe for around $70 per month. The site is basically a forum and blog based group that will keep you up to date on what is taking place within the Affiliate Marketing industry. You will see topics covering New Product Launches and Joint Venture Announcements, JV marketing invites, and articles on marketing and other topics related to the business.

If you would rather be notified by email of upcoming launches, you can join their newsletter, or visit http://www.jointventures.jvnotifypro.com

Once you join the forum every update will be emailed to you automatically. Be careful not to over-subscribe to a multitude of campaigns however, as you'll be inundated with emails.

When writing review pages to promote upcoming launches, there are a few things to consider. First, you want to be honest. If you haven't tried the product, you really can't evaluate whether it's worth the money or not. Just the same, a lot of people can't afford to purchase every big launch that hits the web. So, when creating a review, here are some ways of getting around that:

Rather than talk about your personal experiences with the product, scour the Internet for reviews and feedback submitted by others. Contact buyers and ask if you can use their testimonial on your website regarding that particular product.

If the product hasn't' launched yet and there are no operational reviews available, focus your review on the product developer and previous products he or she may have produced. Talk about the aspects of the product that will benefit the potential customer, discuss the features and showcase any guarantees that are available. Always do your best to provide a thorough description of the product listing both potential pros and cons, otherwise your review may look like nothing more than a way of generating sales. Of course, it may be just that, but no product is perfect; your credibility will be enhanced if you can point out an imperfection or two. What else would you like the product to do? If you can get an advance copy and actually use it, what questions did you have when getting started that were not clearly answered? Was anything confusing? Are the screen colors a little odd? There's something you can find that makes it imperfect. But use the sandwich method—point out a bunch of good things (there must be a bunch or you wouldn't be promoting it), point out a thing or two you would like to see done better, then end with a summary of the good points and why it will help the Internet marketer save time, make more money, or whatever benefits you can identify.

Also keep in mind as you write or record your review, Features and Benefits. People don't buy features; they buy benefits. Point out a feature and then relate it to a benefit to the user.

You never want to be dishonest in a review, nor do you want to exaggerate the product. Not only will you lose sales, but you may end up getting into trouble with the developer. Always visit the developer's website to see what content and graphics are available for you to use. If he or she doesn't have marketing materials to give you, only use the developer's sales materials as a guide and write your own that state the same things *in a different way*. Others will be marketing this same product unless you somehow get an exclusive right to represent the product. You don't want your marketing copy to be the same as someone else's.

Nothing irritates a potential buyer more than reading the very same review on multiple websites. Be sure to put every advertisement, every description including the feature list, into your own words while paying attention that you are accurate in your description. (Of course, some features can't be restated. If a car has 20-inch Z-rated tires, there's really no other way to state this than to repeat it has 20-inch Z-rated tires. Use your judgment and create something that is truthful and your own as much as possible.)

If you're serious about this profession you'll take an online course in ad copywriting. (Take and in-person class if you want.) There's more than one way to say anything. Creativity is the name of the game Make your marketing materials your own.

Your review page should start with a captivating headline. Pull the audience in. Prompt them to read the rest of your review. You also want to include a sub title that continues and emphasizes the theme of your headline and provides just a *little* more information.

The ultimate objective is to get them to click on your affiliate link and purchase the product. In order to increase the chances of that, draw the prospects in carefully. Excite them. Calm their fears (of being scammed, taken advantage of, etc.). Showcase the benefits of how the product will help them make money, save time, be more attractive, or have more fun in life. People have a limited set of deep desires. Appeal to one or more of them and your ad will be like honey to bees.

Another thing to pay attention to is just how many times your affiliate link appears within your review. Advertising is an art, not a science, so there are differing opinions on this.

The first is, while you don't want every other sentence to contain your link, you should focus on making sure it appears numerous times, both within the top section of your article, mid section and bottom/footer area. A good rule of thumb is, two times isn't enough; five times is too many. If you find five link references aren't enough, maybe your ad copy or review is too long. As we've said before, there's a balance in everything. Your readers want information, but if your review gets too long you run the risk of over-delivering and boring the reader. Try to find the happy medium of just enough good information to encourage your prospect to take the next step, going to the sales page and purchasing the product.

If there's a first, there has to be a second. The second theory, and the one I personally subscribe to, is to only include the link to the product at the end of the ad copy. Why? Naturally, you want people to click on your link. But you want even more that those who click are at least interested in what you have to offer. Someone who reads a captivating headline and a few clever lines of ad copy and then clicks on the link may be just web surfing. He's not serious. He just wants to see where you're going. Someone who reads through your entire copy and then clicks on your link is going to be a much better prospect. He's invested some time in your text. Something has grabbed his attention enough to get him to the bottom of the ad. This guy is interested in what you have to offer if your ad copy is honest and sincere. This is the guy you want to click the link.

The lesson? Promote high-quality products and write killer ad copy. (Shameless plug: check out Michael Cheney's [Email BlackOps](#) to learn the secrets of attention-grabbing ads. You may have to [go here](#) first.)

And of course, add an autoresponder form to your squeeze page so that in the event they don't click your affiliate link or buy the product, you at least capture their email so you can follow up with your prospect on other products, send free content to maintain their goodwill, and send other helpful information. "Content is King." If people receive valuable information from you they'll welcome your emails and open them, rather than simply relegating your hard work to the trash folder.

Top five autoresponder service providers:
- Get Response -- https://www.getresponse.com/
- Aweber -- https://www.aweber.com/
- IContact -- https://www.icontact.com/
- eZineDirector -- https://www.ezinedirector.com/
- Mail Chimp – https://mailchimp.com/

As I've mentioned, I began using AWeber upon recommendation of a person who has a huge internet presence. I use AWeber and find it does everything I need at a reasonable price. All the other autoresponders above will do everything you need. Look at their prices and interfaces and decide which one you'll use. Then take the time to learn the ins and outs of their software. Spend time looking at the help page, the community forums, and make yourself an expert in the application. An email autoresponder is to the Internet marketer what the pole is to the pole vaulter.

A Word About Building Your Email List

If you've been in this game for more than about a day you've probably thought about buying an email list. After all, you make a relatively small investment one time for ten-thousand email addresses and you're bound to make some money. Right?

It's true; thousands of contacts are just a credit card swipe away.

But don't do it!

Your marketing will suffer and your brand will suffer. Buying email lists is a legitimate email marketer's kiss of death.

How could this be?

Let's say purchase a list of names and email addresses based on demographic and/or psychographic information. For example, you can purchase an email list of people who have responded to offers for stock market investing advice.

You may, and most likely will, find list vendors who will tell you that their list was created completely from "opt-in" subscribers. This only tells you that the people on the list opted in to an email communication from a *specific* person or company at some *point in time*. What these people didn't do, however, is opt in to receive email communications from *you and your business*.

Consider these facts:

1. Reputable email marketing vendors don't allow emails to email addresses you've purchased.
2. Even if that weren't the case, **good** email address lists simply aren't for sale.
3. Your email deliverability and IP reputation will be harmed if you use the list.

Let's look at point number one in more details.

If you're using and autoresponder or email marketing system now or plan to in the future, you'll find that reputable companies will insist that you use genuine opt-in email lists. You can avoid this little problem by using a non-reputable email marketing vendor. That creates its own problems; ESPs on shared IP addresses that don't require customers to use opt-in email lists typically suffer poor deliverability. One customer's illegitimate email address list can poison the deliverability of the other customers on that shared IP address. So by trying to use a sub-standard, illegitimate autoresponder, you're actually hob-knobbing with the rabble and riff-raff of the internet marketing crowd. You'll end up hobbling your own marketing efforts.

And as for point number two, good email address lists simply aren't for sale. If an address is for sale, it only means that that address has already been ripped up one side and down the other by who-knows-how-many other people who have purchased from the list and repeatedly emailed everyone on it. If an address actually had value in the past, it's been spammed to death by the time it's on a for-sale list. Would you want to buy that?

And consider this; if someone actually had a good email list, wouldn't they keep it to themselves? Personally, I put a lot of time and expense into developing my list. I tell everyone who signs up that their email will NEVER be sold, rented, or shared. My subscribers are like gold and no one, but no one gets them. No respectable Internet marker would want to see the value of their addresses diminished by letting other people get their hands on it. Really, after all the time and expense you go to in order to develop a good email list, would *you* sell it?

And third, people on a purchased or rented list don't know you. They don't know your business and they don't know why you're mailing them or how you got their address. Purchased lists are sometimes scraped from other websites which, I think we can all agree, is a dirty way to acquire email marketing contacts.

But let's say they're not scraped and are acquired through more honest means. After all, companies that sell their lists may tout that their lists are completely opt-in.

But are they really?

Not really. This only means that people who have opted to receive emails from the company they originally gave their address to, not yours. Sure, the opt-in process probably included a statement that said something like, "Opt in to receive information from us, or *offers from other companies we think you might enjoy*," but the truth is that the recipient has never heard of your company, and does not remember opting in to receive emails from you. He or she may not have even read the opt-in statement. This means there's a better than even chance that a lot of the recipients will mark your email as spam because they don't recognize you or remember opting in to communications from you. This results in no sales and, worse, harms your reputation, labelling you as a spammer.

There are businesses dedicated to combating email spam. They set up a thing called a honeypot, is a planted email address that, when harvested and emailed, identifies the sender as a spammer, kind of like an electronic spy. Similarly, things called spam traps can be created to identify spammy activity; they are set up when an email address yields a hard bounce because it is old or no longer valid, but still receives *consistent* traffic. Continuing to send email to a dead addresses is a red flag to these companies. That email address then becomes a spam trap that stops returning the hard bounce notice, and instead accepts the message and reports the sender as a spammer.

If you purchase a list, you have no way of confirming how often those email addresses have been emailed, whether the email addresses on that list have been scrubbed for hard bounces to prevent identifying you as a spammer, or from where those email addresses originated. Are you really willing to risk not only your email deliverability, but also the reputation of your IP address and your company? Even if you find the light after purchasing or renting email lists and decide to only email those who have opted in with your company, it will take you months (or maybe years) to get your Sender Score up and rebuild the reputation of your IP.

It ain't worth it. Build your own list.

How to Grow an Opt-In Email List

So what should you do instead? Grow an opt-in email list. Below are the basic best practices that produce a very big bang for your buck when it comes to consistently growing an email list.

1. Create *gated assets*.

Webinars, eBooks, templates, etc.—these are all good, long-form, premium content assets that people may find valuable enough to give you their email address. The more gated assets you have to put behind landing pages, the better. A wider variety of content will make it easier for you to attract a wider swath of people.

2. Create useful tools.

If eBooks aren't your thing, create tools instead. I don't recommend a one-or-the-other approach, necessarily, but if your talents are more amenable to application development than writing eBooks, this may be a more attractive option for you.

3. Promote those gated assets on your marketing channels.

Now that you have some gated assets that enable you to capture email addresses, spend a considerable amount of time making sure the world knows about them. You have plenty of channels at your disposal—social media, PPC, and email are common tools to turn to. But none will provide lasting returns quite like a well-written, informative blog.

Consider this scenario:

You promote your new gated assets by blogging about subject matters related to the content assets you've created, and then put CTAs that lead to the asset's landing page on every one of those blog posts.

Now let's say, hypothetically, your blog posts get about 100 views per month, and your visitor-to-lead conversion rate on the blog is about 2%. That means you'd get two leads from a single blog post each month.

Then, let's say you write 30 blog posts a month. That means you'd get 60 leads in a month—2 from each blog post. Now keep doing that for a year. The work you did to blog that first month will continue to drive leads throughout the year. That means you're actually getting 4,680 opt-in contacts a month by the end of a 12-month period because of the compounding effects of blogging. We're not talking "get rich quick," but over time you'll develop a valuable list of people interested in what you have to say—and sell.

4. Run creative email marketing campaigns.

Most people don't think of email as a lead- or contact-generating channel. But because people forward helpful emails to colleagues or friends, it can actually expand your database if you simply make forwarding or sharing email content easy for recipients. Include calls-to-action in your emails that make sharing an obvious choice for recipients, particularly with your most useful assets.

Is your list growing mold?

If you already have a large database of email addresses, you also likely have some contacts that have gone quite stale. If so, I recommend running a re-engagement campaign that can help you both scrub your list and prevent the kind of spam and IP issues I addressed earlier, as well as re-awaken old contacts that might have forgotten about you, but would actually be great prospects for sales.

Safelists
We can't leave this section without talking a little about safelists, or safe lists—your preference.

A safelist is a mailing list where all members can mail to each other. These emails cannot be considered as spam because every member has opted in and confirmed his or her email address. They're typically used to advertise websites, business opportunities, and affiliate marketing programs.

When you're a member of a safelist you read ads other people have posted in exchange for the right to post your, which they might read. normally for free. With that said, all safelists allow you to pay for extra advertising, or the ability to pay for additional advertising via emails, banners, and log-in ads without having to click on and read others' emails and ads.

It would seem that a safelist is nothing more than a bunch of people trying to sell to a bunch of people who are trying to sell to those same people. It's more or less like a dog chasing its own tail.

However, because people have to spend a little time on each ad, there's a possibility that if your ad is particularly good or your product is something new and wonderful, you can get a lot of exposure for free or very little expense. Out of the thousands of impressions your ad will get, someone might be interested in it.

It's also the case that someone might sign up for a safelist with one thing in mind, one type of business with some set marketing and promotion ideas, but change his mind along the way or see another angle he hadn't thought of. Sales *are* made through safelists.

In my way of thinking, safelists are one of the ways you can start out and get your brand into circulation. Take some time with your ads, make them engaging and original, and you'll get some traffic.

But beware: most of your traffic will be from people who are clicking your ad to get points toward posting their ads. You may see a thousand clicks at your site, but very possibly you'll have no sales. That's a roundabout way of saying the traffic from safelists is very poor quality.

You get what you pay for.

Seems to me that the greatest value in a safelist is in building an email list of people who are interested in your niche. Post a banner or short email offering a free eBook or other product. The prospect gives you an email and receives a link to the free product.

Everyone's happy.

Sales come later.

Patience is a virtue.

Things to Consider

If you're an affiliate marketer, you're promoting someone else's work by definition, so you want to be particular about the products you promote. Regardless of how much money is involved, you need to show discretion when it comes to tagging your name, your most valuable asset on the Internet, to anything created by someone else.

Be choosy, there is always another big launch right around the corner. If people see that you are careful with the things that you endorse and aren't just jumping on the bandwagon with every other marketer, you will stand out, especially if they are involved in the Internet Marketing industry in some way, shape, or form themselves.

Once you have decided to promote a product, you need to move quickly. Snag as many keyword related blogs as possible (see www.WordPress.com and www.Blogger.com), create a few keyword-related Squidoo lenses (Squidoo.com/your-keyword), create a Hub Page using a relevant keyword, and get going!

You want to have everything set up and in place within four to seven days prior to the launch in order to rank well, and begin to generate traffic.

If you are short on time, find more time. (TV and Internet surfing are time killers.) If that's completely and utterly impossible, focus on, as a minimum:

- Two Squidoo Lenses using two different, but relevant keywords. (Try to get the product name if you can.)
- One Blogger Blog
- One WordPress Blog
- One Hub Page

   Note: HubPages only allows two outbound links, and if you aren't careful to post relevant content (rather than one long advertisement) your Hubpage can be removed without notice.

- One Landing Page

This will help you rank quickly even if you are limited on time. When you register for your blogger account, use the keywords as the site name (example http://Dogtrainingtips.blogspot.com).

The landing page should be hosted on your own website. If you have only one domain name, you can create a sub-domain and host it there (example: dogtraining.yourdomain.com).

If necessary, ask your host how to set up sub domains with your hosting account. For hosting providers like GoDaddy.com, most of their packages come with the ability to create an unlimited number of sub domains at no extra charge.

Your landing page should include specific keyword phrases. Using the Affiliate Shortcut website as an example, I would use:

- Buy Affiliate Shortcut
- Affiliate Shortcut Bonus
- Affiliate Shortcut Review
- Affiliate Code

These keyword phrases have always performed very well for me.

Create Your Blog
Your WordPress blog as well as your Blogger blog should also use these keywords. Here is how to do it:

Visit www.Blogger.com and click on **Create Your Blog Now**.

The first step is to create your account; fill in your name, email address, password, and word verification; then accept their terms (as if you had a choice).

The next page is where you need to be careful. This is where you choose the name of your blog, and when honing in on a targeted product launch, this is where you want to use your keyword string, which should be the product name (if possible).

If it's taken, use a variation or a longer keyword string including the product name, plus reviews (e.g., AffiliateShortcutReview).

I have found that "review" works exceptionally well since most people considering purchasing a product are looking primarily for information about the product from a third party, rather than seeking a bonus or coupon.

The same goes with Hub Pages and Squidoo. When creating a Squidoo lens at http://www.Squidoo.com choose keywords as it will become part of your URL (e.g., www.Squidoo.com/AffiliateShortcutReview would be a great URL with which to promote this product).

Affiliate Shortcut Tips

When creating your Squidoo lens, be sure to take advantage of the various modules that you can include on your page. In addition, break up your content into short articles and avoid linking to any related products until after the initial launch is over, since your focus is on funneling this traffic through <u>your affiliate link</u> to the product's order page.

The great thing about Squidoo lens is that after the launch is over you can easily convert these into general advertising lenses that feature additional products and related services. With Amazon modules, Link Lists, and Text modules you can easily showcase other products or link to other landing pages or blogs that you own, keeping the traffic going to other new launches long after the current one has ended.

Squidoo allows you to set up as many lens pages as you like, so reserving keywords on future launches is a good idea whenever you hear about an upcoming launch. Best of all, creating lens pages takes less time than even creating a blog post, so have fun playing around with the controls.

And last, a lot of people don't realize it, but like blogs, you can ping your Squidoo lens updates. Just visit sites like www.PingGoat.com or www.Pingomatic.com (the two more popular pinging sites) to let the world know that your Squidoo lens is published and updated.

After you have created your blog and have created a few posts (I recommend at least three posts before pinging it) you can generate traffic almost instantly by pinging your blog. You want to use a ping list because it helps the search engines index your content faster, which in turn leads to more people discovering your content and leads to more website traffic.

Here is an extended directory of other free pinging resources:

- http://blogsnow.com/ping
- http://ping.feedburner.com
- http://rpc.technorati.com/rpc/ping
- http://rpc.weblogs.com/RPC2
- http://rpc.blogrolling.com'pinger
- http://blogshares.com/rpc.php
- http://www.blogdigger.com/RPC2
- http://api.feedster.com/ping
- http://www.a2b.cc.setloc.bp.a2b
- http://ping.blo.gs
- http://www.popdex.com/addsites.php
- http://topicexchange.com/RPC2
- http://api.my.yahoo.com/rss/ping
- http://api.moreover.com/ping
- http://rpc.icerocket.com:10080
- http://coreblog.org/ping
- http://xmlrpc.blogg.de
- http://xping.pubsub.com/ping

Please note: you might not want to ping your blog from all of the services above each time you update. It takes some time for all of the services to ping and update, so you may be wasting your time by going to each site. If you update your blog weekly, wait until you have made two or three new posts before going through the ping process. Also note that sites like www.Pingomatic.com

will ping multiple sites for you, including many of the ones on the list above.

When you post to your blog be sure to utilize the ability to add tags to *each and every* one. These tags should include keywords that are relevant to the content in your post If you are promoting a product, be sure to continue to include your keyword phrases such as "product title review."

When you are using a self-hosted blog, you should consider downloading a handful of useful plugins. These are all free and essential in optimizing your blog:

Code Banters' Free Autoresponder Plugin: Automatically inserts an autoresponder code into your blog's template.

>http://www.CodeBanter.com

Share This: Adds an array of social bookmarking sites to your posts allowing your visitors to tag or bookmark your updates.

>https://www.sharethis.com/

The All in One SEO Pack: Helps your blog rank better in the search engines by including titles, descriptions, keywords and other quick blog tweaks.

>http://www.wordpress.org/extend/plugins/all-in-one-seo-pack

Affiliate Cloaking Protection: Affiliate marketers know one thing above all else.

<u>People will steal your commissions every chance they get</u>.

While not everyone is dishonest, and not every potential customer will do this, it only takes one person to remove your affiliate link and go straight to the source. With some programming knowledge, they may even be able to replace your affiliate code with theirs and steal any traffic you have generated.

Thankfully, there are free and easy ways to get around this. One common method is to use URL shortening programs such as:

- http://www.TinyURL.com
- http://ww.SnipURL.com

These programs are free and will not only cloak your affiliate link but they will instantly shorten it (which works well if you use Twitter and other programs that limit the number of characters you can use at once).

The only problem with using these types of services is that the links that are generated are often difficult to remember, since they are a combination of letters and numbers. For those who want an easier, memorable URL to advertise, there's yet another easy solution:

Create a folder on your website called "recommends" or any other name you like such as "reviews," "endorses," "loves," "uses," "likes," etc. This will become part of your new affiliate link.

Now, create a sub directory (another folder within the /recommends one) and call it the name of the product you are promoting. For example, if you were promoting Widgets your URL might be:

> http://www.YourSite.com/Recommends/Widgets

Now, open a text editor and copy and paste the following code, changing the ClickBank link with your own. (Remember, you can generate your new affiliate hop link from within the marketplace.)

<?php

header('Location:http://YourClickbankID.widgets.hop.clickbank.net/?tid=trackthis');

?>

When someone clicks on that link, the text page you created will instantly redirect them to the landing page of the product developers site, giving you full credit should they purchase the product. (Score!) Your affiliate ID and link to the product page are hidden from view so they *cannot* be stolen.

Not only will this easy little trick possibly increase your commissions by avoiding link theft, but your affiliate links will be cleaner and more appealing.

Now, with all that said, there's another, even easier way but it costs a little money. A WordPress plugin called PrettyLinks will allow you to name your product link anything you want in one simple form where you tell it the original URL and give it a URL you prefer. Hit save, and you're done.

One small problem with this is that some services, Udimi.com, for example, limits the number of redirects from a URL. So, let's say you use http://ThisCuteURL.htm to redirect people to http://jvzoo/this-product, which in turn, redirects to the programmer's page, http://MyProduct.html/1234 which then redirects to http://My1234ProductSalesPage.htm, you may have a problem.

If you're intelligent enough to be reading this book, I assume you'll also be intelligent enough to overcome this little challenge by supplying Udimi with the basic link to your JVZoo or ClickBank associate link. Problem solved.

Tip: If your name is available as a domain name consider purchasing it to blend better with yourname.com/recommends

Get the Word Out
With so many social communities available today, it has never been easier for affiliate marketers to cash in on their ability to easily drive traffic to new websites and blogs, build a list, develop a reputation, and establish credibility within Internet marketing circles.

Apart from Squidoo Lens, Hub Pages, WordPress, and Blogger there are dozens of other active communities that enable you to get the word out about your websites and start promoting virtually instantly.

The following social bookmarking sites may seem a bit off the beaten path, but in terms of sending traffic to your website and boosting your rank in the search engines, they are important and often overlooked secret weapons. Just try them out and you'll see for yourself:

- http://www.HumSurfer.com
- http://www.JumpTags.com
- http://www.Mister-Wong.com
- http://www.ClipMarks.com
- http://www.LinksMarker.com
- http://www.LifeLogger.com
- http://www.Bloggingzoom.com
- http://www.Tagos.com
- http://www.Pixel2Life.com
- http://www.Tagza.com
- http://www.Marktd.com
- http://www.Digalist.com

Of course, there are also the giants in social bookmarking sites that you may also want to give some attention to including:

- http://www.Digg.com
- http://www.StumbleUpon.com
- http://www.Waggit.it

Other Ways of Building Links & Generating Traffic Instantly:

Twitter

http://www.Twitter.com

There are countless guides on Twitter marketing, and it's a topic that deserves much more space than I could devote here. Bear in mind that there are no real secrets to harnessing the power of Twitter apart from consistent updates and ensuring that those updates are creative, interesting, and attention-grabbing.

Many marketers merely post links to their blogs or products. With so many posts, a reader will scan right past these without even noticing them. To get attention, post personal tidbits, humorous statements, or interesting remarks that include a link. Important note, don't make every tweet an ad, but by the same token, don't tweet on subjects that may turn potential customers off.

Weebly

http://www.Weebly.com

Create free websites and blogs, switch designs instantly, and features a drag and drop interface, Weebly helps you rank higher in search engines, especially Google.

Article Marketing

Content creation is a vitally important part of affiliate marketing. You can generating traffic to your websites and blogs by writing articles (or outsourcing their creating and publishing them as your own—perfectly legal) and submitting them to e-zine directories like www.EzineArticles.com. Their site says they have almost half a million authors who have shared articles on such topics as gaming, investing, book reviews, insurance, health and fitness, automotive, and just about any other topic you can think of. If you have an expertise, write an article and share it here.

If you don't consider yourself a writer or are just too busy to devote time to writing high-quality articles, you can utilize sites such as Elance.com, Freelancer.com, or Guru.com to find authors who can generate content for you at affordable rates. Remember though, that you get what you pay for. If you buy a 1500-word article for five dollars, you're probably going to have to do some serious editing before publishing it. For a little more, you may be able to develop a relationship with a seasoned writer or two who want to develop a profile and are willing to write at discount prices (initially) in order to receive a testimonial or recommendation from you. (As a writer myself, who has written more than a few articles for virtually pennies, you may consider paying more as your own internet profits increase. C'mon – share the wealth.)

Here is a list of popular article directories that you can submit your content to:

- http://www.GoArticles.com
- http://www.Amazines.com
- http://www.Isnare.com
- http://www.ArticleDashboard.com
- http://www.Articles-Hub.com
- http://www.ArticleTrader.com
- http://www.ArticleAlley.com
- http://www.ArticleSphere.com

- http://www.WebProNews.com
- http://www.Articlesfactory.com
- http://www.ideamarketers.com
- http://www.easyarticles.com
- http://www.kokkada.com
- http://www.articlepros.com
- http://www.articleteller.com
- http://www.selfgrowth.com
- http://www.promotionworld.com
- http://www.biz-whiz.com
- http://www.selfseo.com
- http://www.postarticles.com
- http://www.bigarticles.com
- http://www.neoarticle.com

Naturally, in your articles you'll want to include a link back to your website within your resource box, and update your profile at each article directory to include your name and website URL. You can also feature an author's photo if you would like to better establish an online brand.

To save time and to make life more convenient, you can use an article submission service to automatically submit your articles for you on a regular schedule. One popular resource is available at:

http://www.SubmitYourArticle.com

This popular company will submit your articles to hundreds of e-zine directories for as little as $37.00. They'll also help you to multiply your search visibility by improving your SEO, attract a large audience of engaged, active prospects, and build credibility and authority within your market. Other similar services are SubmitEdge.com and ArticleTrader.com.

Another method of getting your brand in the public sphere is to create short articles and content documents such as quizzes and polls and submit them to sites such as Quizilla.com. When creating your Quizilla account use your product name or website title as your username. Then click on "Make a Creation" to set up your account, and add your article with anchor text (using your primary keywords) that will link back to your landing page, blog, or website.

http://www.Tumblr.com

This is a popular method that affiliates use to generate a quick backlink and beef up traffic. Tumblr is really easy to set up and even easier to use. Create a "tumblelog" within minutes by clicking on the "Sign Up" tab.

http://www.WetPaint.com

Wet Paint features free wiki based websites that allow you to start your own social website instantly, which will help with backlinks, resulting in higher ranking in search engines. Make sure that you click on *Only People I Invite Can Edit My Wiki*" when you create your page so that others cannot modify your links in any way. (Don't forget to do this; I had my pages edited by other marketers frequently until I learned of this option.)

http://www.LiveJournal.com

Another free blog platform that will allow you to customize it from top to bottom including free themes and modules.

http://www.BlogSome.com

This is a free web hosting site for blogs, and allows you to create quick mini blogs instantly using your keywords. You can create as many as you like (reserving as many keywords as you like) within minutes.

http://www.Scribd.com

Create a group or an entire community quickly. Publish your article, add in your links (to your blog or site) and upload it within seconds. Remember to focus on high keyword density but make it readable and interesting.

http://www.Xomba.com

Xomba ranks well in Google and those who create a post on it will see a surge of traffic almost overnight (in some cases in less time than that). Just create your account and upload your 100-200-word article. Use the anchor text-based links so that you are populating your content with relevant keywords and you're good to go.

Directories

Directories are also great for creating a ton of back-links quickly. I have used free directories as a way of generating relevant one-way backlinks by simply submitting my websites and blogs to them every so often.

While not an exhaustive list, this is more than enough to get you started:

- http://www.webolink.com/
- http://www.webde.biz
- http://www.zunchdirectory.com
- http://www.a1dir.com
- http://www.fxe.in
- http://www.placeyourlinks.com/
- http://www.pickedsites.info
- http://www.neonlinks.com/
- http://www.bizgarden.com/
- http://generalbook.info
- http://www.allsitessorted.com
- http://www.deeplinked.com
- http://www.openlinkdirectory.com
- http://www.clickmybrick.com
- http://www.iwebinfo.com
- http://www.e-bizdirectory.com
- http://www.miroweb.com
- http://www.go2directory.info
- http://www.seagency.net
- http://www.all-linkdirectory.com
- http://www.alistsites.com/
- http://www.promotiondir.com
- http://www.discoveryofweb.com
- http://www.linkspedia.net
- http://www.find2k.com/
- http://www.webd1r.com/
- http://www.ipant.com
- http://www.allthelinks.net/

- http://www.100bestonline.com
- http://www.pr3plus.com
- http://www.monsterbacklink.com.ar
- http://www.websitelist.com.ar
- http://www.24directory.com.ar
- http://www.blpdirectory.info
- http://www.freeweblinkdirectory.info
- http://www.linkdirectorysite.info
- http://www.10directory.info
- http://www.powerfulldirectory.info
- http://www.weblister.com.ar
- http://www.extremelinks.net
- http://www.link2.info/
- http://www.linksweb.info
- http://www.topdirectory1.com/
- http://www.ztrixq.com
- http://www.a2zwebindex.com/
- http://www.activedirectory1.info/

Press Releases

These aren't just for the president and major corporations. Press Releases are by far, one of the easiest ways to generate quality backlinks, boost rankings, and generate traffic. I have used press releases time and time again over the years whenever I created a new website that required a jumpstart.

In fact, you can write a press release that goes into circulation within 24 hours for less than $20.00. Your press release should be well crafted, to the point, and not overly lengthy; three hundred to five hundred words is a good length. If you're not experienced in writing press releases, all you have to do is review a few to get an idea of their structure and the information they contain, then model yours in a similar way.

Some press release services are:

- http://www.PRWEB.com
- http://www.WebWire.com

While I prefer the first two, another you might consider using is

- http://www.PRLeap.com.

Top Commentators Tactic
One easy method of generating tons of back links to your blog or website is simply by posting comments on blogs that feature the "Top Commentators" plugin. This plugin ranks contributors based on how many comments they have made. This means that after you have spent a bit of time posting comments on these blogs, your name and website link will appear on every page on their blog in the commentators side-bar. This means that if you find a blog that has hundreds of pages and you end up appearing as one of the Top Commentators, your website will appear on every single one of these pages. Imagine the possibilities for quick (and *free*) back links. Of course, the more authoritative the site, the more valuable your links become.

To help you get started, I have compiled a list of some of the more popular blogs online that utilize the Top

Commentators Plugin. Each of these blogs use the "Do Follow" plugin, which means that your links will be included in search engines.

- http://www.marketingpilgrim.com/
- http://onemansblog.com/
- http://news.filefront.com/
- http://www.shoemoney.com/
- http://vocino.com/
- http://www.searchenginepeople.com/blog/
- http://www.bluehatseo.com/
- http://www.searchenginepeople.com/blog/
- http://courtneytuttle.com/
- http://www.plagiarismtoday.com/
- http://tallfreak.com/
- http://pixelheadonline.com/blog/
- http://www.brandon-hopkins.com/
- http://jakeldaily.com/
- http://www.smartwealthyrich.com/
- http://www.jonlee.ca/
- http://www.venukb.com/blog/
- http://www.wayneliew.com/
- http://www.bontb.com/
- http://onthewebed.com/
- http://www.adesblog.com/
- http://www.Guruslab.com
- http://www.ContentGrab.com
- http://www.BlogRemedy.com
- http://www.johnchow.com/
- http://chenpn.com/
- http://www.ededition.com/

- http://www.bloganything.net/
- http://www.sabahan.com/
- http://bloggingawaydebt.com/
- http://founderscafe.com/
- http://www.bloganything.net/
- http://ahkong.net/
- http://www.blogtrepreneur.com/
- http://www.CashSpark.com
- http://www.GurusLab.com/

Keyword Research & Finding Solid Products

If you haven't already decided on a product mix for your internet business, researching what sells is something you'll want to do. You want to market a product or service you have an interest in, but you also want to market something a million other people are interested in. You may be fascinated by wooden shoes, but if you share that fascination with about a dozen other people in the world you're going to have problems marketing them even with the best of strategies and tactics.

Find out what the public is interested in by conducting a keyword research on specific words and phrases. In other words, if you were searching for your product, what would you enter in a Google (or other search engine) search box? For example, if you were looking for information on toothaches, you might search using this phrase:

"How to stop toothache"

or

"Toothache Home Remedies"

To ensure that your website is found and its URL displayed when someone searches for information related to your business, make sure you use keywords and phrases in your marketing campaigns and website that people are currently searching for. If your keywords are obscure or too technical—words the average joe wouldn't use—your site will not appear in search results and you will lose potential clients or customers.

The easiest and most common method to conducting a keyword research is by using the free keyword search tools available online. Some tools require a membership or monthly payment, and have features and functions that you will find valuable, but when starting out, there are enough resources you can access for free that will give you the information you need to begin earning revenues you can then devote to paid services.

Some free services are:

- Overture Keyword Search (http://inventory.overture.com)
- Google External Search (https://adwords.google.com/select/KeywordToolExternal)
- Good Keywords (http://www.GoodKeywords.com)

If you're so inclined, here are a few pay-for-play services. These are very useful for conducting keyword research and are definitely worth looking into:

- WordTracker (http://www.WordTracker.com)
- Keyword Elite (http://www.KeywordElite.com)

Using Keyword Research Tools

Open up the free Google Keyword Search tool (https://adwords.google.com) to start the keyword evaluation process. When the page loads you will see a search box and the option to search "Descriptive Words or Phrases" or "Website Content."

Choose "Descriptive Words or Phrases."

In the search box type in, for example, "get f at abs" and click on "Get Keyword Ideas."

A search box will appear below with keyword phrases that are related to this search term.

You can click on the drop down menu *"Filter My Results"* and choose to sort by *"Search Volume"* to see the volume of searches conducted using the various keywords and phrases.

The filter options are:

Advertiser Competition: The results under this column show the number of advertisers bidding on each keyword relative to all keywords across Google. The shaded bar represents a general low-to-high guide to help you determine how competitive the ads are for this particular keyword. Greater competition will result in a higher cost should you choose to purchase sponsorship on the Google pay per click search engine (AdWords).

Search Volume: This column shows the search volume for each specific keyword used on Google in the previous month. The shaded bar represents a general low-to-high guide to help you determine, once again, how competitive ad placement might be for that particular keyword.

Average Search Volume: As with search volume, this shows results from past searches. However, this column displays average results over the course of a year, rather than just the previous month. The results table will also show you the estimated cost for advertising using specific keywords as well as an estimation of where your ads will be placed in the sponsor bar on the search results page.

Once you have determined that your keyword or phrase receives a significant amount of searches per month, the next step is to look at the competition and ultimately, how difficult it would be, judging by how expensive the phrase or search words are, to compete with all other users of Google Adwords.

In order to evaluate the cost of running a Google Adwords campaign, you'll need to run another search, this time focusing on the box right below *"Filter My Results."*

Find *"Calculate Estimates Using a Different Maximum CPC Bid,"* and enter $1.00 in the *"CPC Bid"* box. Click *"Calculate"* or *"Recalculate"* to display the results.

As you will see, using the keyword that we previously used, "Get Flat Abs," and setting our maximum CPC to

$1.00, our estimated ad position would be between 1-3, meaning that your Adwords advertisement would show up in either first, second, or third place positioning.

Paying $1.00 per click is expensive for an Adwords campaign, but don't be too concerned; being in the first few positions is not a matter of life and death. Being showcased in a lower position will cost a lot less and can still yield good results with a well-crafted ad and a high-quality.

Another very important thing to note is that regardless of what you choose to spend per visitor on Adwords, you need to ensure that you are making more money than you are spending. While this seems too elementary to even mention, it's easy to get caught up in paying whatever it costs to be in first position. The truth is, the only thing you should be focused on is ensuring that this traffic actually converts at a reasonable rate and that your revenue is larger than your expense. Carefully monitor your stats every day and continue your campaign only as long as it remains profitable.

Further, don't get caught in the *we're losing a little on each sale, but we'll make it up in volume* myth. Again, this seems rather silly, but you'd be surprised at how many people pursue silly propositions when it comes to marketing and business in general. Never give up your rationality, and don't get trapped in the *sunk cost* confusion. Many people will continue to pursue a course of action even when it's apparent that it's not working because they've put *so much money* into it.

Emotionally, they believe that because of what they've already spent they must continue in order to make a success of their earlier decision or marketing plan. But once the money is spent you have a *sunk cost*. The money is irretrievable and continuing a course of action that is leading to failure by all rational calculations, no matter how much you've spent on it, is still leading to failure. Pull the plug. Future decisions should never consider sunk costs; only pursue actions and investment that make sense at this moment, disregarding what has gone before.

And even if you're making a profit on your advertising campaign, you have to consider whether another keyword combination or other service altogether would result in a higher return. A 5% return on investment (ROI) is profitable by definition, but if you're spending your valuable time and resources making 5% when you could be making 10%, you're actually *losing* 5% in *opportunity costs*.

You've found some winning keywords. Now what?
When you have found highly targeted keywords, you can easily go to marketplaces like Clickbank or JVZoo to locate related products that you can promote using these selected keyword phrases. For example, if you found "*Dog Training Secrets*" was a popular search, you could then visit the ClickBank marketplace and use these keywords in your product search. Then, choose from the list of available products and set up your landing page to showcase that product with a review. From your review, link to the merchant's page.

Final Words

Making money as an affiliate marketer can be an enjoyable experience as long as you create a plan of action and take steps to follow through. Don't get lost in the many traffic generation techniques out there, or the countless product launches that breeze through your inbox promising the world for a song. Focus on one thing at a time, utilize the methods and resources found within this guide and supplement it with _continued training_. Tools and techniques change daily You can't learn the trade then sit back for the next ten years, or even one year, and continue raking in profits. This is a game of constant learning and adaptation.

Enjoy the process. The money will follow.

Internet Marketing Glossary

Note to readers: Many of these definitions borrow heavily from Direct Online Marketing, (https://www.directom.com/) but a definition, by definition, is simply a definition, not subject to creative license, at least in my humble opinion. I have limited the verbiage to the minimum required to define the term and have made additions and corrections where necessary. You can find out more about any of these terms by searching on Direct Online Marketing, Wikipedia, Google, Bing, and countless other Internet locations.

A

Above the Fold - The part of the page you can see without scrolling down or over. The exact amount of space will vary by viewer because of screen settings. You often pay a premium for advertisement placements above the fold, which will add to the costs of internet marketing services, but may also add to results.

adCenter - Bing Ads powers paid search results on Microsoft's Bing, Yahoo! (as of November 2010), and other sites within its network. Bing Ads was formally known as Microsoft adCenter.

Ad Extensions - Added information that is included in your text ad. These can include extra features about your business, such as your location, phone number, links to certain product or services pages, and call-outs.

Advertising Network - A group of websites where one advertiser controls all or a portion of the ads for all sites. A common example is the Google Search Network, which includes AOL, Amazon, Ask.com (formerly Ask Jeeves), and thousands of other sites. In Google AdWords, they offer two types of ad networks on the internet: search and display (which used to be called their content network).

AdWords - AdWords is Google's paid search marketing program, the largest such program in the world and in most countries with notable exceptions such as China (Baidu) and Russia (Yandex). Introduced in 2001, AdWords was the first pay per click provider offering the concept of Quality Score, factoring search relevancy (via click-through rate) along with bid to determine ad position.

Affiliate Marketing - A type of internet marketing in which you partner with other websites, individuals, or companies to send traffic to your site.

Aggregate Data - Data that details how a group of consumers interacts with your marketing efforts or websites. This can be how an audience views videos, ads, pictures, etc. and what actions are taken after viewing. This can give a comprehensive view of how your target market is engaged, as a whole, through marketing efforts, as opposed to individualized consumer data.

ALT Tags - HTML tags used to describe website graphics by displaying a block of text when moused-over. Search engines are generally unable to view graphics or distinguish text that might be contained within them, and the implementation of an ALT tag enables search engines to categorize that graphic. There is also talk that business websites will all be required to utilize ALT tags for all pictures to comply with certain American Disability Act requirements.

AMP - An acronym for the Google-backed Accelerated Mobile Pages Project was announced by Google in October 2015. It was designed as an open-source initiative for publishers to create content that loads quickly on mobile devices. AMP consists of three parts: AMP HTML, AMP JS & Google AMP Cache. For more information see the [AMP Project website](https://www.ampproject.org/) (https://www.ampproject.org/).

Analytics - Also known as Web Metrics. Analytics refers to the collection of data about a website and its users. Analytics programs typically give performance data on clicks, time, pages viewed, website paths, and a variety of other information. The proper use of Web analytics allows website owners to improve their visitor experience, which often leads to higher ROI for profit-based sites.

Anchor Text - The clickable words of a hypertext link; they will appear as the underlined (usually) blue part in standard Web design. In the preceding sentence, "hypertext link" is the anchor text. As with anything in SEO, it can be overdone, but generally speaking, using your important keywords in the anchor text is highly desirable.

Astroturfing - The process of creating fake grassroots campaigns. Astroturfing is often used specifically regarding review sites like Google Places, Yelp, Judy's Book, and more. These fake reviews can be positive reviews for your own company or slander against your competitors. Generally frowned upon, to put it mildly, by ethical Internet marketers.

Automated Rules - A feature in Google AdWords that automatically adjusts your ad statuses, budgets, and bids based on the specific parameters that you set.

Average Position - This statistic describes what position in which your ad typically appears on the search results page.

B

Backlinks - Links from other websites pointing to any particular page on your site. Also called Inbound Links. Search engines use backlinks to judge a site's credibility; if a site links to you, the reasoning goes, it is in effect vouching for your authority on a particular subject. Therefore, Link Building is an incredibly important part of Search Engine Optimization. How many links, the quality of the sites linking to you, and how they link to you all are important factors in ranking your web site on search engines.

Baidu - Serving primarily China, Baidu is the largest non-US based search engine in the world (although it was started in the United States). Sites can be optimized for Baidu and they offer their own paid search service.

Banners - Picture advertisements placed on websites. Such advertising is often a staple of internet marketing branding campaigns. Depending upon their size and shape, banner ads may also be referred to as buttons, inlines, leaderboards, skyscrapers, and other terms. When using specifics, banner ads refer to a 468×60 pixel size. Banner ads can be static pictures, animated, or interactive. Banner ads appear anywhere on a site. Banner costs vary by website and advertiser; two of the most popular pay structures are Cost per 1,000 Impressions (CPM) and flat costs for a specified period of time.

Beacon Technology - is a form of technology that allows companies, primarily retailers and marketers, to connect and engage wirelessly with consumers via their mobile devices. The appeal is that companies can use the Bluetooth signal to deliver geo-targeted, personalized messages, and push notifications when the customer is in range of the beacon, and can even act as an analytics tool to decipher steps taken to reach a purchasing decision.

Behavioral Targeting (BT) - Behavioral targeting tries to put ads in front of people who should be more receptive to the particular message given past Web behavior, including purchases and websites visited. The use of cookies enables online behavioral targeting.

Bing - Bing is Microsoft's search engine, which replaced live.com in June 2009. Bing results now power Yahoo!'s search for paid (except display; through Microsoft adCenter) and organic (except local listings) through an alliance between the two companies.

Bing Ads Editor - Bing Ads Editor is a free downloadable application for managing Bing Ads advertising campaigns. It allows the advertiser to manage multiple accounts at the same time, make bulk changes, copy or move items between adgroups and campaigns, and more.

Bing Merchant Center - Bing Merchant Center is a tool that helps you upload your store and product data to Bing and make it available to Bing Shopping.

Black Hat SEO - The opposite of White Hat SEO, these Search Engine Optimization, or SEO, tactics are ways of tricking the Search Engines to get better rankings for a website. Black Hat SEO is a temporary tactic for increasing ranking, as search engine designers are constantly on the lookout for techniques that attempt to circumvent their algorithms. If not immediately, using black hat methods will eventually get your site drastically lower rankings or banned from the search engines altogether.

Blog - Short for Web log, blogs are part journal, part website. Typically the newest entry (blog post) appears at the top of the page with older entries coming after in reverse chronological order.

Bounce Rate - The percentage of people who visit your website but leave without visiting any other page.

Brand Stacking - Multiple page one listings from a single domain. Prior to 2010, a site would be fortunate if it had three first page results for branded searches. Since Google tweaked its algorithm to include Brand Stacking, that number has risen to as many as eight of the top search rankings

Broad Match - This is the default matching option. With this bid type your ad may show if a search term contains your keywords in any way. Your ads may show for synonyms of your keywords, related searches, and other relevant variations or phrases.

Buyer Persona - Fictional depictions of your target customers that serve as valuable points of reference for various digital marketing strategies. Marketing professionals take considerations from buyer goals, industry research, customer data, demographics, and natural human behaviors when forming buyer personas. The ultimate goal of this practice is to create an image of your ideal customer. That way, you can personalize your site layout, develop new content, or tailor any marketing strategies to increase the chances of acquiring the customers you need to grow your business.

C

Canonical Tag - A canonical tag tells (most) search engines which page is preferred when two URLs are similar or duplicate. In most instances this tag is used when you have products or content that is accessible by multiple URLs or in some cases, even websites. The tag is part of the HTML head code using the attribute *rel=canonical*.

Cascading Style Sheet (CSS) - Defines how HTML elements such as layout, colors, and fonts will be displayed. External style sheets can be stored in CSS files which allow for faster loading pages, smaller file sizes, and other benefits for visitors, search engines, and designers. A style sheet helps to maintain a unified look and feel, thus a more professional appearance throughout all pages of your web site.

ccTLD - ccTLD's are "Country-code" TLD's showing what country a site is focused on or based in. Using Google and the United Kingdom as an example, Google UK is google.co.uk. Sometimes these ccTLD's are two sets of letters separated by a period (e.g. "co.uk" for the UK or "com.au" for Australia) and sometimes they are just one set of letters (e.g. ".fr" for France).

Click through Rate (CTR) – The formula (number of clicks) divided by (number of impressions) gives the click through rate, a common internet marketing measurement tool for ad effectiveness. This rate tells you how many times people are actually clicking on your ad out of the number of times your ad is shown.

Cloaking - Showing a search engine spider or bot one version of a Web page and a different version to the end user. Several search engines have explicit rules against unapproved cloaking.

Content Management System - Content Management Systems (CMS) allow website owners to make text and picture changes to their websites without specialized programming knowledge of software like Adobe Dreamweaver or Microsoft FrontPage. CMS examples include WordPress, Drupal, and Joomla.

Content Marketing - Content marketing is an inbound marketing practice that seeks to generate leads and traffic through the creation and distribution of content that caters to the needs of a defined audience of prospective customers. Content marketing as a strategy for SEO service providers achieved critical mass in the latter part of 2012 following the release of the Penguin algorithm update by Google, which adjusted a number of spam factors and affected a high percentage of search queries.

Content Network - Each major search engine offers a form of a content network within its paid search interface, typically referred to as content networks, although Google just renamed their content network the Google Display Network.

Content Tags - HTML tags such as Header and Alt Tags that define the essence of the content contained within them.

Contextual Advertising - A feature offered by major search engine advertisers allowing your advertisement to be placed next to related news articles and on other Web pages. Contextual advertising seeks to match Web content from the display page with your advertised search term(s).

Conversion Rate - This statistic, or metric, tells you what percentage of people is taking an action the advertiser defines as a conversion. A "conversion" may mean, for example, a sign-up for free information, a completed survey, or a purchase.

Conversion Rate Optimization - Depending on what your site deems as a conversion, there are steps that can always be taken to improve the likelihood that visitors to your site will perform a conversion driven action. Typically, this means changing certain aspects centered on the conversion. For example, if you have an ecommerce site, you may change the orientation of certain elements or their physical appearance like the color of the "Add to cart" button or removing certain steps to make it easier to purchase an item. Conversion rate optimization relies heavily on A/B testing as what may work for one website may not necessarily work for another.

Cookie - a small piece of data sent from a website and stored on the user's computer by the user's web browser while the user is browsing. Cookies were designed to be a reliable mechanism for websites to remember stateful information (such as items added in the shopping cart in an online store) or to record the user's browsing activity (including clicking particular buttons, logging in, or recording which pages were visited in the past). They can also be used to remember arbitrary pieces of information that the user previously entered into form fields such as names, addresses, passwords, and credit card numbers.

Cost per Acquisition (CPA) - An online advertising cost structure where you pay per an agreed-upon actionable event, such as a lead, registration, or sale.

Cost per Click (CPC) - A common way to pay for search engine and other types of online advertising, CPC means you pay a pre-determined amount each time someone clicks on your advertisement to visit your site. You usually set a top amount you are willing to pay per click for each search term, and the amount you pay will be equal to or less than that amount, depending on the particular search engine and your competitors' bids. Also referred to as Pay Per Click (PPC) or Paid Search Marketing.

Cost per Impression (CPM) - A common internet marketing cost structure, especially for banner advertising. You agree to pay a set cost for every 1,000 (M in Roman numerals) Impressions your ad receives.

Crawler - Component of a search engine that gathers listings by automatically "crawling" the Web. A search engine's crawler (also known as a Spider or robot) follows links to Web Pages. It makes copies of those pages and stores them in a search engine's index.

Customer Relationship Management (CRM) - Software solutions that help enterprise businesses manage customer relationships in an organized way. An example of a CRM would be a database containing detailed customer information that management and salespeople can reference in order to match customer needs with products, inform customers of service requirements, etc.

D

Day Parting - Day parting refers to serving ads at different times of the day and days of the week, or even changing bids or ad copy at different times. For example, you may not want your ads to show from 11AM-2PM on Tuesdays. This can be done manually in most online platforms, or automatically in some such as Google AdWords.

Description Tags - HTML tags that provide a brief description of your site search engines can understand. Description tags should contain the main keywords of the page it is describing in a short summary.

Display URL - The URL displayed along with your ads. This URL can vary from the Destination URL, but must use the same root domain.

Directories - A type of search engine where business listings are gathered through submissions, information pulled from data aggregators (e.g. Acxiom), or a combination of the two. Websites are often reviewed and placed in a relevant category. Directories can be utilized for strengthening local SEO and providing relevant referral traffic.

Domain Authority - Developed by Moz (Moz.com), domain authority is a score ranging from 0 – 100 that predicts how a website will rank on search engines. It is often used by SEOs to compare one site to another as well as tracking the improvement over time.

Domain Name - A website's main address.

Doorway Page - A Web page created to rank well in a search engine's organic listings (non-paid) and typically delivers very little information to those viewing it.

Domain Name Monitoring - Monitoring Domains across various extensions. For example, a monitoring service may keep metrics on the domains MyName.com, MyName.net, and MyName.Biz.

Drip Marketing - marketing communications that are written in advance of delivery, and then sent to prospective customers or current customers at pre-determined intervals in their buyer or customer journey.

Dynamic Retargeting - Ads shown to users who have already been to your site. These ads typically contain images and information about the previous item viewed.

E

EdgeRank - The algorithm Facebook uses to rank business / brand pages, groups, celebrity pages or individual accounts to determine which posts from those accounts will appear in the Newsfeed of users connected to those pages and profiles (or pages and profiles tagged in the posts).

E-Marketing - Another synonym for online marketing, internet marketing, or digital marketing. Marketing strategies (like SEO, PPC, retargeting, social advertising, etc.) that are deployed using web based technology in an effort to generate sales leads or e-commerce revenue.

Enhanced Bidding - A feature specific to Google AdWords. When you select to utilize enhanced bidding, you're giving AdWords the power to adjust your bidding in order to increase conversions.

Exact Match – Refers to keyword search matching. This is the most specific of the match types. With this type your ad or page will only show if the user's search term contains your keywords exactly as they are written.

Expanded Text Ads - Text ads with double the characters compared with standard text ads. The ad format (today) is composed of two 30-character headline fields, one 80-caracter description field and two 15-character paths in the display URL field. ETAs are mobile-optimized, so you can reach potential customers on desktop and mobile devices with the same ad.

F

Final URL - The URL address for the page to which you're sending traffic from your ads.

Folksonomy - also known as social tagging, is a user-defined metadata collection. Users do not deliberately create folksonomies and there is rarely a prescribed purpose, but a folksonomy evolves when many users create or store content at particular sites and identify what they think the content is about.

Forum - A place on the internet where people with common interests or backgrounds come together to find information and discuss topics.

G

Geo-Targeting - The ability to reach potential clients by their physical location. All the major search engines offer the ability to geo-target searches in their Pay-Per-Click campaigns by viewing their IP addresses. Geo-targeting allows advertisers to specify markets by regions as far as IP address can identify them.

Gmail Sponsored Promotions (GSP) - Google Display Network campaigns that allow advertisers to show ads in Gmail. The advertiser pays when someone clicks to expand the ad in their inbox.

Graphical Search Inventory - Banners and other types of advertising units that can be synchronized to search keywords. Includes pop-ups browser toolbars and rich media.

Growth Hacking – Not a specific technology, but a way to increase customer acquisition using the most effective tactics available to engage a specific buyer persona. Typically deployed in the "Software as a Service" industry or startup environments, growth hacking often involves multiple marketing strategies and nimble product development practices to create a solution that rapidly scales the user base of a product/service.

H

Hashtag - Formerly called the 'pound sign', this symbol (#) is used on social media (primarily Instagram and Twitter), as a way to group tweets or pictures by category or phrase. The '#' is placed directly, without space, in front of the text to be marked.

Header (or Heading) Tags () - HTML heading and subheading tags are critical components of search engine marketing, as often times both are graphical, thereby unreadable to search engine spiders. Optimally, page titles should also be included to clearly define the page's purpose and theme. All of the header tags should be used according to their relevance, with more prominent titles utilizing <h1> (heading 1), <h2> (subheading), and so on to <h6>.

HTML - HyperText Markup Language, the programming language used in websites. Developers use other languages that can be read and understood by HTML to expand what they can do on the Web (e.g., Java, Javascript).

Hyperlink - Typically blue and underlined, hyperlinks, commonly called "links" for short, allow the user to navigate to other pages on the Web with a click of the mouse.

I

Image Maps - Clickable regions, hyperlinks, within images displayed on a web page. Image maps enable search engine spiders to "read" this material.

Impressions - The number of times someone views a page displaying your ad. Note that this is not the same as actually seeing your ad, making placement and an understanding of the site's traffic particularly important when paying on a Cost per 1,000 Impressions basis.

Inbound or Incoming Links - See Backlinks

Inbound Marketing - Marketing services and strategies that successfully cause prospective customers to navigate to a website on their own accord, usually due to the consistent creation of engaging content. Examples include SEO, content marketing, blogging, and email marketing to a list that is self-curated. This is in contrast to traditional advertising methods that get the attention of prospective customers through paid advertising promotions.

Index - The collection of information a search engine has which searchers can query against. With crawler-based search engines, the index is typically copies of all the Web pages they have found from crawling the Web. With human-powered directories, the index contains the summaries of all the websites that have been categorized.

Internet Marketing — A catch-all phrase that includes any of a number of ways to reach internet users, including Search Engine Marketing, Search Engine Optimization, and Banner advertising.

Internal Linking - Placing hyperlinks on a page to other pages within the same site. This helps users find more information, improve site interaction, and enhances your SEO efforts.

Interstitial - An ad that appears between two pages a person is trying to view. The ad often appears near a hyperlink allowing someone to quit viewing your ad and go directly to the page he or she originally tried to access.

J

JavaScript - Not to be confused with its distant cousin Java, Javascript is an Object Oriented Programming language developed by NetScape. It provides enhanced functionality over and above the capabilities of HTML.

K

Keyword - Almost interchangeable with Search Term, keywords are words or a group of words that a person may search for in a Search Engine. Keywords also refer to the terms you bid on through search engine marketing in trying to attract visitors to your website or Landing Page.

Keyword Difficulty - A metric commonly used in search engine optimization that determines how much on-page targeting and offsite link building will be required to rank for a phrase. Also commonly referred to as KPI, most tools that monitor keyword difficulty use a percentage scale of 1-100, with phrases ranked in descending order.

Keyword Stuffing - When the Web was young and search engines were starting to gain in popularity, some smart website owners realized that the search engine algorithms responded better to some meta tags than others, so they started overusing these keywords, often with high search volumes and no relevancy to the site, into the title, description, and keyword tags.

Keyword Tags - HTML tags that define the keywords used on web pages.

L

Landing Page - The first page a person sees when coming to your website from an advertisement.

Link Building - The process of obtaining hyperlinks (links or backlinks) from one website back to your own.

Link Juice - SEO term referring to the equity passed to a site via links (either internal or external). High authority, high traffic sites have more link juice, which will more positively affect your rankings, than a low authority, low traffic site. The more link juice your site has, the more positively the search engines will view it.

Link Popularity - How many websites link to yours, how popular those linking sites are, and how much their content relates to yours. Link popularity is an important part of Search Engine Optimization, which also values the sites that you link out to.

Link Reclamation - This is when outreach is performed to earn backlinks to your site. The situations in which this occur can be if your domain name changes, a re-branding occurs, or when your brand is mentioned online (in an article, blog post, etc.) and there is no link from the mention going back to your website.

Local Search - A huge and growing portion of the search engine marketing industry. Local search allows users to find businesses and websites within a specific geographic range. This includes local search features on search engines and online yellow page sites. Optimizing for local search requires different practices than for traditional Search Engine Optimization.

Long Tail Keywords - a keyword phrase that contains at least three words (though some say two or more is considered long-tail). Long-tail keywords are used to target niche demographics rather than mass audiences. In other words, they're more specific and often less competitive than generic keyword terms.

M

Marketing Automation - Software suites that combine a variety of popular online marketing strategies like email, social media, CRM and SEO into one platform. In addition to efficient and automatic completion of a variety of marketing tasks, these applications also allow marketing teams to view a more direct correlation between their efforts and ROI from online marketing.

Meta Search Engine - A search engine that gets listings from two or more other search engines rather than crawling the Web itself.

Meta Tags - (see also keyword tags, description tags etc.) – Meta tags allow you to highlight important Keywords related to your site in a way that matters to Search Engines, but that your website visitors typically do not see. Examples of meta tags include Header Tags and Alt Tags.

Microblogging - Microblogging refers to platforms allowing you to post information in snippets of 140 characters at a time via phone or web. Twitter is the preeminent example of a microblogging site, although there are many others, such as Gab (Gab.ai).

Microsites - a site created by a business or online publisher, for a specific purpose, that functions independently from the primary website of the business/publisher. Microsites are typically created for events, specialized topics or services, or for content created for a specific topic.

Mobile Enabled Website: Also called Mobile Optimized Website. This is a version of your website that is built to display correctly on internet enabled smart phones such as the iPhone. Mobile Optimized Websites offer an easier to read and navigate platform for users and scales down images for viewing on a smaller screen.

Mobile-Friendly - A site that is optimized for mobile users. The text and images must be able to be viewed on a display on a mobile device while still being functional and user-friendly.

N

Natural Listings - Also referred to as "organic results", these are the non-advertised listings in Search Engines.

Naver - Naver is Korea's largest search engine and Web property.

Neuromarketing - A field of marketing that incorporates neuroscience as a means of predicting consumer behavior.

O

Opt-in - This type of registration requires a person submitting information to specifically request he or she be contacted or added to a list.

Organic Listings - See Natural Listings.

Outbound Links - Links on any web page leading to another web page, whether they are within the same site or another website.

P

PageRank - PageRank is a value that Google assigns for pages and websites that it indexes, based on all the factors in its algorithm. Google does release an external PageRank scoring pages from 1-10 that you can check for any website, but this external number is not the same as the internal PageRank Google uses to determine search engine results. All independent search engines have their own version of PageRank. Potentially interesting fact: PageRank was named for Google's Larry Page and it is calculated at the page level – pun fun!

Paid Inclusion - Advertising program where pages are guaranteed to be included in a search engine's index in exchange for payment.

Paid Listings - Listings that search engines sell to advertisers, usually through paid placement or paid inclusion programs. Contrast with organic (natural) listings.

Paid Search - Also referred to as Paid Placement, Pay Per Click, and sometimes Search Engine Marketing, paid search marketing allows advertisers to pay to be listed within the Search Engine Results Pages for specific keywords or phrases.

Pay-for-Performance - Term popularized by search engines as a synonym for pay-per-click, stressing to advertisers that they are only paying for ads that 'perform' in terms of delivering traffic, as opposed to CPM-based ads, which cost money, even if they don't generate a click.

Pay per Click (PPC) - a business model whereby a company that has placed an advertisement on a website pays a sum of money to the host website when a user clicks on to the advertisement.

Permission Marketing - focuses on receiving the consent of users before being contacted or, in some cases, even seeing an advertisement (see also Opt-in). Permission marketing is centered on the concept that people are increasingly tuning out the barrage of advertisements they see each day. Its focal tenet is that a business will have a better chance of gaining a client when the client first gives permission to be sent an ad or contacted.

Phrase Match - This match type is more specific than broad, but not as specific as exact. This bid type allows your ads to show for phrases that exactly contain your keywords or are close variations.

Pop-Under - An advertisement that opens in a new Web Browser window once you visit a particular page or take some other action. Considered less annoying than Pop-Up ads because the new window appears behind the existing one.

Pop-Up - An ad or web page that opens a new window on your screen that partially or wholly covers your current web browser window.

Push Notifications - are messages that pop up on mobile devices, that originate from a specific app or server. It's not necessary to be using your mobile devices, or even be in the app, to receive push notifications. They act as a way to keep the user engaged with the app, and hopefully take action (ex: send a coupon, event notification, etc.).

Q

Query - Query is another term for "keyword" or "search term." Within Google AdWords, search query reports show the actual terms that searchers used to click on your ads, as opposed to the advertised keyword that is in your account. These two sets of words may or may not be the same.

R

RSS Feed - Rea Simple Syndication (RSS), also Rich Site Summary, originally RDF Site Summary; often called Really Simple Syndication, is a type of web feed that allows users to access updates to online content in a standardized, computer-readable format.

Reciprocal Link - A link exchange between two sites. Both sites will display a link to the other site somewhere on their pages. This type of link is generally much less desirable than a one-way inbound link.

Remarketing - Remarketing is Google AdWords's term for retargeting

Responsive Ads - Responsive ads automatically adjust their size, appearance, and format to fit just about any available ad space. For example, your responsive ad might show as a native banner ad on one site and a dynamic text ad on another, as it automatically transforms itself to fit precisely where you need it to go to meet your advertising goals.

Retargeting – Directing advertising to a person based on information about sites he or she has previously visited. When a user performs an action (e.g., a visit to a site or a search) a cookie may be placed on his or her browser. As the user visits other sites, advertising, such as a banner or other type of display ad, is shown on their display based on information stored in the cookie.

Return on Investment (ROI) - A performance measure used to evaluate the efficiency of an investment or to compare the efficiency of a number of different investments. ROI measures the amount of return on an investment relative to the investment's cost. To calculate ROI, the benefit (or return) of an investment is divided by the cost of the investment, and the result is expressed as a percentage or a ratio.

Rich Media - Web advertisements or pages that are more animated and/or interactive than static Banners or pages.

Robot or Bot - See Crawler.

Robots.txt - A file used to keep Web pages from being indexed or to tell which pages you want a search engine to index.

Root Domain - The term root domain means different things depending on whether it refers to the Internet as a whole or a specific website. Your root domain commonly means the highest level of hierarchy for the website you control. MyName.com is the root domain for MyName.com/Blog, MyName.com/Store Front, MyName.com/About, etc.

Run of Site (ROS) - A contract specifying Run of Site means that a Banner or other type of online advertisement can appear on any page, and usually in any open placement, of a particular website.

S

Schema Markup - a piece of code added to a page's HTML code to help search engines understand what your website is about and what type of information it contains.

Scraping - The process of copying content from one Web property and using it on another. In other words, stealing. Scraping technologies have evolved because of the needs for current, relevant content and to stay ahead of legitimate content creators trying to protect what they've written.

Search Engine Optimization (SEO) – Using writing and programming techniques to make a site more "search engine friendly." The end result is making a site appear higher in search engine rankings.

Search Engine Reputation Management (SERM) - This allows a person or organization better positioning through strategy involving Search Engine Optimization, Paid Search Marketing, Press Optimization, Blogging, and Social Media.

Search Engine Results Page - Search Engine Results Pages, or SERPs, are the Web pages displayed by any Search Engine for any given search. They display both Natural (organic) Listings and Pay-Per-Click ads. How high you are listed and where your ad is shown depends on Search Engine Optimization; and paid Search Engine Marketing respectively.

Search Retargeting - A specific type of retargeting that allows an advertiser to show ads to searchers of given keywords who have never visited the advertiser's site.

SEM - An acronym for Search Engine Marketing and may also be used to refer to a person or company that does Search Engine Marketing – either paid search, search engine optimization, or both.

SEO - An acronym for Search Engine Optimization and may also be used to refer to a person or company that does search engine optimization.

Shopping Ads - Formerly known as Product Listing Ads (PLAs), these ads appear in both Google and Bing search results as images of individual products above the search results. These ads are specifically for eCommerce companies and instead of using keywords, ads are triggered by searches containing words in the product's title, description, or attributes.

Signature –A few lines of default text that can be customized and added to all outgoing email messages from a personal email account.

Site Retargeting - The most common form of retargeting, this refers to displaying your ads to a visitor based on a visit to your site, or individual page of your site. These cookie-based ads can appear on any publisher's page throughout the ad network being used. Various targeting options exist, including only showing ads when a certain page has been visited (such as a landing page) and an action has not been completed (e.g. a conversion).

Social Commerce - Selling goods directly online through social media channels. As "electronic commerce" was shortened to "eCommerce", social commerce is sometimes shortened to "sCommerce" or "fCommerce," the latter being short for "Facebook commerce."

Social Media - A type of online media where information is uploaded primarily through user submission. Web surfers are no longer simply consumers of content, but active content publishers. Many different forms of social media exist including more established formats like forums and blogs, and newer formats such as wikis, podcasts, social networking, image and video sharing, and virtual reality.

Social Media Marketing (SMM) - An online marketing mix that utilizes the different strategies available through social networking sites to promote a product or service.

Social Networking - A type of social media, social networking websites allow users to interact and create or change content on the site. These sites, which businesses are now using for marketing purposes, allow users to create their own websites and/or online spheres (e.g. LinkedIn and Facebook), share photographs (e.g. Flickr), microblog small bits of information to their personal community (e.g. Twitter) or recommend information for others to find on the Internet (e.g. del.icio.us and Digg). The sites in this last grouping are also referred to as social bookmarking or social news sites. There are also a growing number of sites that are heavily dependent on mobile and geographic locations, such as foursquare.

Spam - Can refer to unwanted data sent via email or put on a website to game a search engine. Spam to a search engine is Web content that the search engine deems to be detrimental to its efforts to deliver relevant, quality search results.

Spider – As a spider might crawl over a web, World Wide Web spiders "crawl" this web to find all the linked pages of a website to gather information to include the site in their natural listings and to determine each site's ranking vis-a-vis various search terms.

Stickiness - How often people return to a website. Constant updates, news feeds, and exclusive content are all ways to make a site stickier.

Structured Snippets - These ad extensions allow your ads to highlight specific aspects of products and services. They provide context on the nature and variety of your products and services before visitors click through to your site.

Subdomain - Also referred to as a 3rd level domain is very simply, a domain that is part of a higher domain in web hierarchy. Subdomains can be created at any time with no limit and without a registrar. A common reason to create subdomains would be to differentiate a sector of your business such as "info.yoursite.com" or "tools.yoursite.com."

Submission - The act of submitting a URL for inclusion into a search engine's index. Unless done through paid inclusion, submission generally does not guarantee listing. In addition, submission does not help with rank improvement on crawler-based search engines unless search engine optimization efforts have been undertaken. Submission can be done manually (i.e., you can fill out an online form and submit) or automated, where a software program or online service may process the forms behind the scenes.

Subpage - A page that appears below the top-level pages in a website's navigation. These pages often appear as drop downs in a top navigation bar or sidebar menu. Think of subpages as "child pages" of the "parent page."

T

Tags - Words or phrases used to describe and categorize individual blog posts, videos, and pictures. Correctly using tags organizes content for users and can help with visibility through SEO and social media optimization.

Takeover Ads - A type of display advertising typically reserved for high profile brands and products (consumer goods, new mass media releases, sporting events) on high traffic online publications. Commonly referenced on the homepages of sites like Yahoo!, MSN, or even ESPN.com, this advertising strategy is often called a "homepage takeover."

Targeting - Shaping internet marketing campaigns to attract certain specific groups of prospective clients. Examples of groups that might be targeted include women, gun owners, and Medicare recipients. Behavioral Targeting is a newer, specific type of focus for advertisers

Topic Modeling - An SEO strategy used when creating or optimizing content based on the primary keyword selected for a page. This is done by identifying keywords related to the same subject of the primary keyword and utilizing these as secondary keywords. Content is then optimized around the new keywords, achieving a higher level of SEO.

Text Ad - An online advertisement that contains only written copy. Paid listings found on the results pages of the main Search Engines are currently Text Ads.

Three Way Linking - A link building strategy designed to create two one-way links between sites that want to complete a link exchange. When using this link-building tactic, one website owner involved in the exchange of links typically has access to more than one property. After adding an external link from one site (in this example, "Site A") to another destination ("Site B"), then Site B places an external link to a third domain ("Site C"). Therefore, a three way link exchange is completed when Site A links to Site B, and Site B links to Site C.

TLD - Top Level Domain. The last segment of a domain name, or the part that follows immediately after the "dot" symbol. TLDs are mainly classified into two categories: generic TLDs and country-specific TLDs. Examples of some of the popular TLDs include .com, .org, .net, .gov, .biz and .edu.

Tracking Code - Information typically included in the URL that allows an advertiser to track the effectiveness of various aspects of an advertisement. Commonly tracked items include Search Term and referring Search Engine.

TrueView Ads - A video ad created in Google AdWords. TrueView video ads come in two formats: in-stream and in-display. In-Stream ads appear before videos on YouTube (owned by Google) and the Display Network. In-display ads can appear in YouTube search results, videos, or on partner websites.

Twitter Retargeting - Twitter Tailored Audiences are used to create retargeting campaigns that can serve ads to people who have previously interacted with your brand.

U

URL - Uniform Resource Locator. These are the letters and symbols that make up the address of specific Web pages, e.g., http://www.demarsouthard.com.

Unique Value Proposition (UVP) - In essence, what it is that sets your product, service, or company apart from others.

Universal Search - The placement of multiple types of results within a general search so that a user receives images, videos, local search results, news articles, and more next to general Web pages. Also called blended search.

Usability – A measure of how easy it is for a user to navigate a website and find the information he or she is seeking.

User-Generated Content - Brands with a dedicated audience will sometimes try to include them in the content creation process. Known as user-generated content, or "UGC," users or community members of a brand will create and contribute their original content for the brand. This content is usually posted via social media or directly on the brand's website.

V

Video Marketing - An online marketing strategy that leverages the consumption of videos by internet users to promote a brand, product, or service.

Viral Marketing - A newer method of internet marketing that attempts to make advertisements so interesting that viewers will pass them along via social networking sites to others free of charge to the advertisers.

W

Web 2.0 - Web 2.0 was never clearly defined, but focuses on several major themes, including AJAX, social networking, folksonomies, lightweight collaboration, social bookmarking, and media sharing. Wikis and user-edited search all operate under this premise.

Web 3.0 – Not completely accepted by the industry, this term refers to the third generation of web technology, focusing on innovation in back-end infrastructure. It is expected that this cycle will continue for five to ten years, and will result in making the Web more connected, more open, and more intelligent. The term was coined first by John Markoff of the *New York Times*.

Web Browser - An application used to access the internet. Common browsers include Microsoft Internet Explorer (IE), Apple's Safari, and Mozilla Firefox, and Google Chrome.

Webinar - "Web Seminar". These virtual seminars allow people from anywhere in the world to attend via an internet connection. They offer tremendous opportunities for businesses to reach out to people over large geographic areas at low costs.

Web Metrics - See Analytics.

White Hat SEO - Used to describe certain Search Engine Optimization (SEO) methods, being "white hat" means using only SEO techniques that are completely above board and accepted by the Search Engines.

WordPress - WordPress is an extremely popular Content Management System. Developed originally for blogs, WordPress offers a great degree of flexibility and functionality.

WYSIWYG – Acronym for *"What You See Is What You Get"*. Usually refers to an interface where you can edit a file, whether it's an email message or a brochure. "A WYSIWYG interface".

X

XML - Extensible Markup Language. Content developers use this language with a variety of forms of content, including text, audio, and visual in order to allow users to define their own elements.

Y

Yandex - Yandex is a search engine serving primarily Russia and other countries formerly part of the Soviet Union. They also offer a Google AdWords-like paid search program, Yandex Direct.

www.ingramcontent.com/pod-product-compliance
Lightning Source LLC
Chambersburg PA
CBHW070146230526
45471CB00002B/542